Baja Bound

To Cabo and Back

Taggart George

Far and Away Publications
Pollock Pines, California

Published and Distributed by:
Far and Away Publications
P.O. Box 283
Pollock Pines, CA 95726
www.farandawaypub.com

Printed in the United States of America

Library of Congress Control Number: 2006925799

ISBN 1-4243-0228-5
    978-1-4243-0228-4

Acknowledgements

I would be remiss if I didn't thank everyone who made this book possible. I am amazed how much help I needed to get *Baja Bound* to press.

I would like to thank Kat, my traveling companion, wife, and ardent supporter in everything I do. We have had so many adventures together, and I hope to have many more with you. It wouldn't be the same without you. You have spent many afternoons alone without complaint while I plunked away on the computer, trying to make words flow onto the paper. Your support of all my crazy schemes has made all the difference.

A special thanks to Kristen Bahlmann, who has spent many hours poring over the many drafts of this book. I know it was a Herculean task to try to fix all of my punctuation and grammatical mistakes. Without your help everyone would have known how little I learned in grammar school.

Thanks to Gary Peterson, who encouraged me to publish and finish the book myself. A little encouragement from someone in the business makes all the difference. Your creative efforts in the cover design and help with the interior maps were also appreciated.

In conclusion I would like to thank my parents, Brenda and Bryan, for their constant support in all my endeavors. You guys have always believed in me and given me the tools that I needed to succeed.

Many have helped along the way, and I appreciate their efforts.

Disclaimer

Sometimes there is very little separating a wonderful adventure from a complete disaster. The smallest detail can completely change the outcome of an entire trip. We were fortunate in our travels across Baja to avoid major catastrophe. While we planned and educated ourselves as best we could, I admit that a substantial portion of our good luck was nothing more than that—good luck. There were many times, if things hadn't gone our way, that the outcome of our trip could have been very different.

I hope everyone who travels in Baja will enjoy the same good luck, but that won't always be the case. Travel with caution and use good judgment. Sometimes my poor decision making led to harsh consequences. May you learn from my mistakes and not repeat them.

This book is not intended to be a guidebook. It is a story of adventure and discovery. If you feel inspired to travel in Baja, try one of the accurate and detailed guidebooks mentioned in this book.

I have done my best to supply accurate information in this book but apologize in advance to Baja aficionados who will surely find small errors. I cannot accept any liability for any loss, injury, or inconvenience sustained by any traveler as a result of information contained in this book.

Let the adventure begin. . . .

Introduction

I licked my parched lips and let the oars drop deep into the current. Standing up on the seat, I scanned the river ahead. I could hear the dull roar of the rapid around the bend echoing off the canyon walls. Taking a quick swig of water from my Nalgene, I reviewed my run in my head: find the marker rock, take the channel to the left, hit the hole, and then pull to the right.

"Is this a big one?" asked Charles, one of my passengers.

"You won't be disappointed, I can promise you that," I replied.

The thick muddy water of the mighty Colorado River swirled around our large Maravia raft, and its placid appearance masked the enormous power below the surface. Just around the next bend the smooth calm water would transform into a snarling cataract of white water, studded with rocks and huge recirculating hydraulics.

I looked back at the other two rafts trailing behind me, their bright yellow rubber in sharp contrast to the chocolate-colored water and the brilliant red-rock canyon walls above. I let my oars dangle just above the water's surface and waited for Kat's boat to catch up. "You want to pull over and scout it?" I called.

"Nah, let's just go for it," was the reply, as she sunk her oars into the current and pulled ahead.

As we rounded the bend, the roar of the rapid filled the canyon and the river disappeared over the thin straight horizon line, indicating a sudden elevation drop. Over the horizon line I could see white spray and foam dancing on the crests of huge waves. I did a quick check to make sure all the dry bags and gear were strapped down securely and once again stood up on my seat to find the marker rock. My passengers squirmed and looked around for a secure handhold in preparation for the rapid. "Well folks, hold on tight and we will try to get through this thing right side up," I said with a smile.

Up ahead Kat was setting up for her entry into the rapid. Finding the marker rock was sometimes difficult at this water level, and I could see her scanning the river as she approached the rapid. Dropping back into her seat she gave two powerful strokes on the oars, pivoting the boat and dropping over the edge into the rapid. My passengers' eyes grew large as the eighteen-foot raft disappeared below the horizon for a couple of seconds before rocketing out of the huge hole, only to disappear again into another monster hydraulic.

Finding the marker rock, I squared up to the first huge hole and accompanying wave and we dropped over the edge. Planting my oars deep in the underlying current, we crashed into the ten-foot standing wave. The front of the boat was inundated under mountains of white water, and I pushed on the oars with all my might to maintain our forward progress. I could barely hear the passengers' shrieks of delight and yells of excitement over the thunderous roar of the water as we dropped into the next hole.

Gallons of water filled the bottom of the boat, overwhelming the self-bailing feature as we sloshed through the rapid. After the next wave I pulled hard on the right oar, spinning the boat and pulling to the right to avoid the treacherous rock pile downriver. We followed the wave train around the rocks and hit several more standing waves before finding ourselves back in calm water. Catching my breath, I looked up at the tall canyon walls and the beauty of the river that carved them and reminded myself that I was *actually* being paid to do this.

The pop of sizzling pine sap brought me back to reality and I blinked my eyes, refocusing and seeing the flickering fire for the first time in several minutes. The warmth of the wood stove felt nice against the winter chill, and I could see snow falling outside the window. Although it has been several years since I worked on the river, sometimes it seems like it was only yesterday. Even now all I have to do is close my eyes to instantly find myself floating on the river. The memories, experiences, and lessons I learned during those carefree summers have shaped my adult life.

It was on the river that Kathryn, affectionately called Kat, and I first met, and the river became a central part of our relationship. We worked together, spent time together, and played together. After a summer on the river, we dated all winter and were married at the end of the next summer. We continued to work the river together for several seasons, but as we finished college we had to move on to more full-time employment.

The nomadic lifestyle of seasonal work was difficult to leave, and it was hard for us to settle down. Working on the river opened my eyes to the fact that there was much more to life than a nine-to-five job. There was so much to see and do in the world, and it was all mine for the taking if I could only manage to find a way to earn a living without sacrificing all of my time. Surely that sort of job shouldn't be too hard to find, right?

So with these lofty ideals and dreams, Kat and I headed out into the real world to seek our fortune. We moved around for a couple of years while I finished my education, and we eventually found ourselves living in northern California. I had just started a job that was nearly perfect: it paid the bills but still gave me enough time off to enjoy life. We bought a house, and before we knew it we seemed to be settling into bona fide real life — the very thing that I had been trying to avoid for so many years.

On this particularly grey and cold wintery afternoon, as I sat daydreaming about the river, it hit me like a ton of bricks that I had done it: a career job, a monthly mortgage, and a mountain of bills — I was in it up to my neck! This was what awaited me for the next twenty-five years. Don't get me wrong, I liked my job and our house, but it all seemed so final. There wouldn't be any more summers on the river or a prospect of relief from the grind of life for quite a while.

Winter has always been hard for me. Maybe it's the lack of sunlight or the cold. Whatever the reason, during the winter I find myself getting antsy and dissatisfied with wherever I am and whatever I'm doing. It must be some remnant of a prehistoric migratory instinct that surfaces every fall and grows stronger as winter progresses, eventually taking over my subconscious. To avoid going crazy or actually quitting my job and moving somewhere new every winter, I try to keep my mind occupied by reading about exciting and far-away places. This seems to quiet my urge to fly south and makes life more bearable for those around me who have to listen to my craziness.

Adventure and travel books are a lifesaver during the winter. By curling up with a good book I can vicariously soak up another's adventure. I sit enthralled as tales of far-off places and exotic destinations fill the hours. I have traveled to all seven continents, summited the highest mountains, and sailed the rolling seas—all while turning the pages of a book. These books give me needed escape and fill the void that winter brings.

I have often found myself dreaming of following in the authors' footsteps, but too many times the sheer magnitude of their undertakings has overwhelmed me. Stories of rafting the Amazon, motorcycling across Asia, backpacking the Appalachian Trail, homesteading in Alaska—they all get me pumped up until I remember that my so-called "real life" might get in the way.

Many of these epic trips just don't seem possible for a regular guy like me. I like to keep an open mind, but almost all of these world travelers have made some sort of monumental personal sacrifice to accomplish what they have done. Some of them postpone starting a career, while others actually quit their current jobs to follow their dreams. As much as I want to follow their example, I know that the cost of quitting my job and altering our lives permanently is too great. Yet countless times after finishing a particularly good book, the thought lingers: "Maybe, just maybe, I could swing something like that."

Conception

One bleak December afternoon I finished reading a book by Tim Cahill entitled *Road Fever*, in which he documents his involvement in a race to set the new world record for the fastest drive from the tip of South America to the farthest northern point in Alaska. The book details his whirlwind journey as he and a friend complete the drive across the American continents in only twenty-three and a half days. Spellbound, I found myself anxiously turning pages, engrossed in the race. The more I read, the more excited I got about the idea of a mega road trip. How awesome would it be to drive the length of South America?! My imagination was sparked, and I was feeling inspired.

Maybe, just maybe, such an adventure was possible for Kat and me . . . but on a slightly scaled-down version. Maybe it *would* be possible to escape out from under our responsibilities, at least for a few weeks, and hit the road. The thought of a brief respite from the routine had some real appeal. Realistically we probably wouldn't be able to drive across South America, but there were certainly other options. The seed had been planted in my brain, and it was only a matter of time before it grew and blossomed.

As I mulled around the idea of an international road trip adventure, it became apparent to me that the destination would have to be Baja California. It just popped into my mind like a bolt of lightning: we should drive the whole length of the Baja Peninsula! This trip had all of the right elements—it was outside of the country, had a tangible goal to reach, and best of all it was warm and sunny down there.

I had been to northern Baja once several years prior during Christmas break. Kat and I, along with two of my college buddies, took a quick road trip into northern Baja. We were only able to spend three days there and didn't make it very far south of the border, but we had a fantastic time. Driving into Mexico felt foreign, exciting, and maybe even a little bit dangerous. The little taste I had gotten of Baja had left me wanting more.

The more I thought about it, the more I knew that the southernmost tip of Baja should be our destination. Miles of desolate coastline, rugged desert, and sunny weather all screamed to me that this would be the place. Best of all, this type of adventure would be feasible. Baja was reasonably close—only a day's drive from our northern California home. Also, the border is fairly easy to cross, and I had heard of people driving the whole length of the peninsula before. I was pretty sure that this was actually something we could do.

My knowledge of Baja was rudimentary at best, and I wasn't even sure how long the peninsula was or how many days it would take to drive down and back. The truth was, I didn't know what this sort of road trip would actually entail, but I figured the details would work themselves out as we went along. I was inspired, excited, and ready to start planning.

It was amazing how quickly my winter blues faded away with that fateful decision. It is important to note that this epiphany was realized, inspiration received, and decision made in a matter of a few hours— all while Kat was away at work. By the time Kat had returned home from work, I had ordered two separate guidebooks on Baja and spent several hours looking at Baja web sites. I was able to find out pertinent information such as the actual mileage from the border to the southern tip and a few other important pieces of information that confirmed that this trip would be possible.

As I announced "our" new plan to drive the Baja peninsula in the spring to Kat upon her arrival home from work, she tentatively agreed to get excited about the plan. She has learned to be understanding of my bursts of "inspiration," as this wasn't the first time such a thing had happened while she was away at work.

A winter or two ago I started to feel the wanderer's itch something fierce. I tried to ignore it, but it just wouldn't go away. I was finishing up my paramedic program and was tired of school. I was only a month away from completion, and the next step was to seek employment as a paramedic. After an intensive year of paramedic school, I was worn out and not eager to start such a demanding job right away.

One afternoon while Kat was at work, it suddenly came to me that we should to move to Alaska for the summer. I had always wanted to live in Alaska, and there seemed no better time than the present to start planning it out. This would give me the break I so desperately needed, and I could always get a job as a paramedic after we came back.

I got busy on the Internet and selected several companies that might hire us as summer employees. A few hours later I had sent off several letters of interest to prospective employers with our resumes attached — all while Kat was at work. Kat took the news pretty well that evening and agreed to the plan. A few months later when spring arrived, we packed up just about everything we owned into our Explorer and set off for Alaska. Our summer in Alaska is a story for another time, but as I said before, winter is a hard time for those who dream of far-off places.

Preparation

I anxiously awaited the arrival of the guidebooks I had ordered. Each day I checked the mailbox and cursed the UPS truck as he drove past our house without stopping. A week or two later when they finally arrived, I soon became immersed in making plans for Baja. I devoured the books, spending hours reading and rereading them, highlighting useful information, and taking notes. The guidebooks that I used while planning the trip were: *The Magnificent Peninsula, Hidden Baja*, and *AAA's Baja California*. Each book had its own strong points and specific emphases that made them unique. By using the books together, I got a very complete overview of what to expect. I must have read them all cover to cover several times.

Over the next few months I gathered more books, maps, and all the information I could find on Baja. I found myself getting frustrated because I would get so amped up about the trip and then remember that it was still months away. January and February seemed to drag on and on, but having a light at the end of the tunnel made all the difference. I found myself daydreaming about far-off places like La Paz, Bahía Concepcion, and Cabo San Lucas. Even shoveling snow became much more bearable while thinking of sunny warm beaches along the Sea of Cortez.

After poring over the different guidebooks, I determined that the ideal time for us to head south would be late April and early May. I picked this time to go for several reasons. One of the main reasons was that the crowds of tourists that flock to Baja in the winter would be gone. Another factor was the weather. I hoped that by going during the early spring months we would avoid the scorching summer temperatures but still have water that would be warm enough to swim and kayak in. Also, my one year of probation with the fire department would be over, and it would be easier to arrange to take time off once this was completed.

By using two days of vacation and lining up several shift trades, I would be able to string seventeen days together for the trip. This would give us fifteen days in Baja with a couple of days on either end to drive the length of California. Several of the guidebooks gave rough itineraries that ranged from ten to twenty days for driving the length of the peninsula. According to my research sixteen days would afford us enough time to enjoy the trip down and not have to rush back up.

Unlike Tim Cahill in *Road Fever*, I had no aspirations of setting a speed record but rather wanted to see and do as much as possible on the way down and back. As the time grew closer to leave, I agonized over whether I should try to take more time off, but in the end we decided that sixteen days would be plenty.

Before I knew it the winter months had slipped by and the trip was getting closer and closer. We needed to make final preparations, buy supplies, and gather together our gear. As the time to leave grew closer, Kat started to get more excited and involved in the planning. We spent a good deal of time planning and preparing to leave in the final weeks before the departure date.

Although some people might find all the preparations needed for such an expedition tedious, we had a great time planning out the trip together. All the planning and preparation that we did for the trip became an integral part of the adventure. Half the fun is in the planning. . . . Well, not really half, but a good portion of the enjoyment and satisfaction derived from taking such a trip is experienced during the dreaming, scheming, and planning stages.

Kat and I pored over the different guidebooks together, extracting useful tidbits of information. We would each take a guidebook, look up a certain city or region, and find the interesting things to see and do. Then we would select the places and activities that looked fun to us and write a quick note on the map near the proper area. We used simple abbreviations to note which book it came from, along with the page number. Soon the map had numerous markings such as: *canyon hike, pg. 297, MP* or *free beach camping, pg. 196, HB*. We used a different color ink for each book's notes to make it easier to differentiate from which book the information came.

This system made it easy for us to pull out the map, look at a certain area or town, and have a quick overview of what there was to do there. While on the road we could reference the details quickly by looking them up in the appropriate guidebook. Soon our map was covered in multicolored notes detailing all the camping spots, points of interest, and things to do in each area. This method of marking the map and using the guidebooks as references turned out to be exceptionally helpful during the trip.

Because we were traveling more than a hundred miles south of the border, we had to jump through several legal hoops to comply with Mexican law. First we had to purchase Mexican auto insurance and obtain a special letter of permission to take the vehicle out of the country. Once the truck was legal, we then had to make sure that we wouldn't have any problems crossing the border. Kat dug out our passports and made sure that they were still valid, along with our original birth certificates. These documents would be necessary to get a Tourist Card, which is similar to a travel visa. Once across the border we could present our identification at a special government office, pay a fee, and then be issued our Tourist Cards. With these cards we would be free to travel up and down the peninsula.

We hammered out a rough budget for the trip, factoring in how much money we would need for gas, food, and lodging. The bulk of the money was allotted for gas. I tried to estimate roughly how many miles we would travel and then calculated how many gallons of gas we would use. Once I had that figure, I then had to do a little research on the price of gas in Mexico. Petroleum products in Mexico are regulated and distributed by government-run gas stations, called Pemex stations, so prices don't fluctuate much, which made it easier to come up with an accurate estimation of how much we would spend on gas.

We planned to bring a lot of our food with us but knew that it would also be fun to eat locally. We planned to use the food from home to cook breakfast and dinner and to mainly eat out for lunch; thus our food budget was modest. This would give us the benefit of familiar food most of the time but the opportunity to also experience the local cuisine.

Our plan was to camp most nights, spending only an occasional night in a hotel to get cleaned up. Most of the camping would be free, although sometimes we would have to stay in a camping area that had a small fee. All in all we planned on spending less than 1,200 dollars on the whole trip

We decided to exchange most of our cash into Mexican currency prior to leaving, thus eliminating the hassle of exchanging money along the way. In addition, we took one hundred dollars in small bills in case some places would only accept dollars. We were a little nervous about having such a large amount of cash, so we planned to split it up and hide it in several different places in the truck. Having a good chunk of the money that we would need in pesos turned out to be advantageous, because we didn't have worry about paying for things with dollars and hoping that we were getting a fair exchange rate. Also, by treating the sum of money that we took out before leaving as all we had for the trip, we avoided overspending.

With any large expedition you have to purchase supplies and equipment. I bought a sit-on-top double kayak for Christmas in anticipation of the trip. It was a bit of an impulse buy, but we really enjoyed it during the trip. We already owned most of the basic camping supplies we would need but had to purchase a few extra items such as a kayak rack for the truck, extra gas cans, and water jugs. Overall I don't think we had to spend much more than 100 dollars buying new gear for the trip, excluding the kayak and kayak rack.

We weren't sure how easy it would be to buy food in some of the more remote locations, so we decided that it would be wise to bring a substantial amount of food with us. Packing food for a fifteen-day trip can be daunting, but fortunately Kat has had lots of experience over the years packing food for long river trips. She spent days organizing all the food into separate large storage containers, which we ended up calling Tupperwares. Each Tupperware was packed carefully according to what meal it contained. Breakfast, lunch, dinner, and snacks all had their separate Tupperwares to facilitate easy access to the appropriate items. The kitchen and cooking utensils had their own separate container as well. This system of Tupperwares turned out to make our lives much easier during the trip, since we had to load and unload everything each day.

As the piles of gear lying on the floor of our front room grew and grew, it became apparent that space in the truck would be precious. We had stacks of Tupperwares, camping gear, the kayak, snorkeling accessories, plus all of our clothes. Worried about possible theft of items left in the bed of the truck, we had to try to fit as much as possible in the back seat of the truck. To gain extra room we ended up taking the back seat out of the truck. By doing so we were able to fit the majority of our gear inside the cab.

With only a few days to go we started to pack the truck up. It was a challenge to fit everything inside in a manner that was both organized and efficient. I felt like we were playing a gigantic game of Tetris. We had a pile of different shaped objects that all had to fit together perfectly to fill the space. After several tries we finally came up with a way where everything fit neatly.

Time to leave, at last. I was buzzing with excitement as I walked around the truck doing a quick check to make sure everything was ready to go. Tupperwares and duffels filled the back seat, while the gas cans, water jugs, and our mini BBQ were strapped in the back. Atop the truck sat the kayak, glowing a dull yellow in the strong sunlight. After months of anticipation, the time had finally arrived!

We turned the water off, checked that all the windows were shut, locked the front door, and pulled out of the driveway. We made it about a block from the house before we pulled over and ran through a quick mental checklist to make sure we hadn't left anything lying on the kitchen counter that we would need. We did a quick check and decided that it was all there. "Yup, we've got it all . . . or we'll make due without it," we agreed.

Speeding south on the interstate, I could feel it— freedom! Freedom from work, our responsibilities, and real life . . . at least for a few weeks. We looked at each other and smiled: it was time for another adventure together.

The endless miles of the fertile central valley slipped behind us one at a time as we left "real life" farther and farther behind. On the highway I caught the jealous glances of several passing motorists as they eyed our setup, and I could tell that they longed to join us.

The destination for this evening was my parent's house in southern California. The plan was to get a good night's rest, awake early, and cross over into Baja.

Map of Days 1, 2, and 3

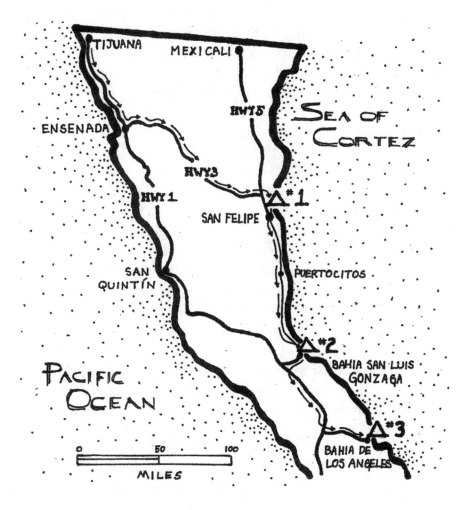

Day 1

We spent the night with my folks in southern California and awoke early the next morning. Before leaving Kat and I attended to the final preparations. We topped off Jerry cans of water, filled coolers with ice, and tucked away odds and ends. We said our goodbyes and hit the road, leaving anxious family members behind.

Traffic was unusually light by southern California standards, and several hours later we neared the border. After waiting in a short line, it was our turn and I pulled up to the window. The border guard got out, looked over our rig, and asked a few perfunctory questions before waving us through. Not two minutes after crossing the border I managed to get us hopelessly lost, and we soon found ourselves driving around downtown Tijuana.

One would think that the way to the major highway running the length of the peninsula would be clearly marked once you cross the border, but both times I have been to Baja I have gotten lost immediately after crossing the border. There is a confusing mess of turnoffs and signs with large arrows that inconclusively point the direction to follow. Before I knew it the turnoff that I selected abruptly ended and dumped us into the heart of downtown Tijuana.

The streets were crowded, and everyone was driving like they were fifteen minutes late for a very important appointment. A thin sheen of sweat broke out on my forehead as I nearly rear-ended a bus while trying to drive and decipher the confusing road signs at the same time. Horns blared behind me as I made yet another abrupt lane change. Kat tried to be helpful by pulling out the map and yelling such things as "turn here," "slow down," and "watch out!" My personal favorite was when she repeatedly shouted, "You missed the turn!" After a few stressful minutes and a couple of near accidents, we finally found the right signs that led us to the proper road and fled the city.

I was able to calm down once we were out of the city and on the open highway, and we settled in for a scenic drive. This section of Highway 1 follows the coastline and is an easy drive with two lanes in either direction. One of the reasons the road is so wide and in such good repair is that every few miles there is a tollbooth where you have to pay a toll of several dollars to proceed.

We had driven this section on our previous trip into Baja, so it was familiar to us and almost seemed like an extension of southern California. This stretch of coast is very developed, with beach houses, hotels, and other buildings lining the coast. Every once in a while there is a patch of undeveloped coastline, but usually there is a large sign announcing what will be built there in the near future.

An hour or two later we reached the bustling city of Ensenada, which is Baja's third largest city and has become a popular tourist destination. Its proximity to the border and pleasant climate make it an ideal weekend getaway for those who live in southern California. The town sports many luxury beach resorts and is a popular stopover for cruise ships.

The majority of American tourists who drive across the border in their own cars never stray farther south than Ensenada. Ensenda offers the perfect mix of familiar and foreign to make most tourists feel comfortable. On the one hand there is the ever-present feeling of adventure in the air, knowing you are traveling in Mexico, but the knowledge that the border is only a short drive away puts the mind at ease.

We stopped in the city of Ensenada to obtain our Tourist Cards. As mentioned earlier, the Tourist Card is required if one is going to travel south of Ensenada. I was worried that it might be a hassle, but it turned out to be very easy to obtain. The office was clearly marked with a large sign outside, and the gentlemen behind the counter helped us right away. All we had to do was fill out a short one-page form, show our passports, and fork over forty dollars.

After getting our cards, we walked over to the waterfront to eat some lunch. We had marked on the map a street that had good outdoor restaurants and decided to go find it. Even with a map of Ensenda right in front of me, I managed to get confused and lost. After wandering around for ten or fifteen minutes, I eventually figured out that we were already *on* the street we were looking for. (Not a really auspicious start for someone who is embarking on a sixteen-day road trip through a foreign country.) Chagrined, I relinquished my decision-making privileges to Kat, and she selected a restaurant. She chose well and we ate some killer fish tacos—a wonderful introduction to Baja's cuisine.

A huge cruise ship was anchored out in the harbor, dwarfing the local fleet of small fishing boats. Its presence was overpowering and we were excited about the prospect of leaving the tourist influence behind. Enjoying the pleasant afternoon, we walked along the marina, looking at the sailboats and watching the fishermen unload their catch.

Just south of Ensenada we turned off of Highway 1 onto Highway 3 heading east. During our previous Baja trip we had traveled a short distance on Highway 3 before taking a side road off toward a remote mountain lake called Laguna Hanson. We soon passed the road that led to the lake and found ourselves in brand new territory. Our destination for that evening was the coastal town of San Felipe. It was exciting to finally cross into the unknown, and it marked the beginning of the real Baja adventure.

The drive over to San Felipe was spectacular. Highway 3 winds its way up and over a large mountain range that divides the west coast from the east. These craggy mountains run down much of the peninsula like a jagged spine. The foothills are mostly devoid of vegetation, and boulders the size of Volkswagen Beetles dot the valleys and hillsides. Dry riverbeds crisscross the valley floors, and the occasional yucca sprouts up between the rocks.

We were surprised to find several fertile valleys tucked up between the barren peaks. These pockets of irrigated land support large alfalfa fields and small farming communities. These green valleys seemed out of place in the otherwise barren landscape.

As we drove farther into the mountains, we started to notice rusted out cars and trucks abandoned alongside the highway every so often. At first we didn't think anything of it, but after seeing the fourth or fifth one, we started to get a little concerned. Many of them were flipped upside down and looked as if they had been lying out in the sun for years. Some looked like they had been in horrible accidents, while others were riddled with bullet holes. All had been stripped of anything of value, and the empty shells were left to rot in the desert.

We pondered the phenomenon silently for a few minutes, hoping to come up with an acceptable explanation that wouldn't make us nervous. Kat finally asked, "What do you think is up with all those cars?" Unsure of what to make of it, I made some silly comment about how the drivers of those cars must have forgotten their AAA cards. We both laughed, a little nervously, and I adjusted my grip on the steering wheel and scanned the horizon for possible hazards. We definitely weren't in Kansas anymore.

As the sun got lower in the sky, we caught our first glimpse of the Sea of Cortez. At first all we could see was a thin silver ribbon on the horizon. I was stoked, to say the least. I had been dreaming about the Sea of Cortez for months now, and it was finally in view. I soon forgot about all the rusted out cars that we had seen along the highway and got excited about what lay ahead of us.

Descending out of the mountains onto the dry coastal plain, the landscape grew more desolate, and the shimmer of water in the distance grew larger and larger. I rolled down my window, and the smell of salt and tumbleweeds filled my nostrils. A few miles later we reached the junction where Highway 5 meets the 3 and we turned right, heading south toward San Felipe.

We found a campground off the main highway a few miles outside of San Felipe. To reach it we had to drive for a mile or so down a sandy dirt road leading to the beach. Every so often we would hit a patch of soft sand, and I had to gun it as we slid across the soft spot. I was a little nervous driving across the sandy patches at first, but we were always able to regain traction on the other side, so I started to feel more confident about the truck's ability to handle the sand.

We were met with a dazzling sunset of fiery orange, which reflected off rivulets of seawater that braided the tidal flat. The tide was out and a wide mud flat stretched for several hundred yards till it met the water. Several palapas and picnic tables stood on the sandy beach, along with several dilapidated beach shacks. (Now for those of you who are unfamiliar with palapas, they are sunshade shelters made of driftwood supports with a roof of thatched palm fronds.) The campground was deserted, actually abandoned by the look of things, and we had the place to ourselves. It was everything that I had been dreaming about all winter: the soft sand, brilliant sunset, and sparkling water—I was hooked.

Looking around we picked the best spot to camp with the nicest palapas and picnic table, which as fate would have it was about thirty feet down the beach. I had made it across the sandy patches on the road without too much difficulty, so at the time driving on the beach seemed like a good idea . . . turns out it wasn't.

Kat was a little hesitant about driving on the beach and got out. She walked across the beach scouting out the best path to reach our camping spot. Even with my limited knowledge of how to drive in sand, I figured that having some good momentum would be helpful. I put the truck in reverse and rolled back a few feet to get a running start. At first the sand appeared to be sufficiently firm, so I kept advancing out onto the beach and figured I could make it over to the camping spot without any problems.

Things were going fine for the first ten feet or so, but once I passed the point of no return, the truck slowed, the tires started to spin, and I settled to a lurching stop. Not having much experience driving in sand, I did what any self-respecting gringo would do—I gunned it, hoping to regain my momentum. Turns out this was also a bad idea. The back tires only sank lower into the sand and continued to spin helplessly, spraying sand out behind me.

By this time Kat was running back over waving her arms. With a sinking feeling in the pit of my stomach, I rolled down the window and asked what she thought we should do next. "Stop giving it gas and get out," she panted. This seemed reasonable, so I turned the key off and got out to inspect the damage. The back tires were nearly buried up to the axle. At this point I realized that things were going to get worse before they got better.

Trying to be optimistic, I made some dumb comment like, "No problem, it will only take a few minutes to dig it out." It was apparent that Kat wasn't impressed with my optimism or my decision to drive out onto the beach. She looked both worried and angry about our current predicament. I would like to say that this was the first time in our relationship that I have ignored good advice and gotten myself into trouble, but unfortunately that is not the case. From prior experience I knew that Kat was not going to be happy about this. She hates it when I do stupid things like this.

While planning this trip I had given some thought to the fact that we were taking a two-wheel drive truck on a trip where four-wheel drive would be helpful. Buying a new truck was out of the question, so my solution to this dilemma was buying a tow strap, a small shovel, Fix-A-Flat in a can, and then hoping for the best. It was nice to see that my planning was already paying off on the very first day of the trip.

So, axle deep in the sand, I got down to business. I took out the shovel and started digging. The plan was to dig out the axle, place the floor mats of the truck underneath the tires for traction, and then back out. Kat was trying to be helpful and not act mad, but I could tell she was pretty unimpressed with the progress I had made while trying to free the truck.

Several hours later I was sweating, covered in sand, and, of course, the truck was still firmly stuck. Meanwhile I had managed to trash our floor mats, excavate a sizeable hole, and was now running out of ideas on how to free the truck by myself. It was time for the back-up plan — the tow strap.

Walking up the beach in the dwindling twilight, I rehearsed in my head the Spanish phrase for "stuck in the sand." There were lights on in several beach houses down the way, so I headed in that direction. Lucky for us, someone was home. It was Sergio to the rescue. "Sí, I have a 4x4 truck," and, "Sí, I would be willing to come pull you out." He was no stranger to the antics of foolish gringos on the beach and knew exactly what to do. I was extremely relieved to find help so quickly and apologized profusely for bothering him as we drove back toward our camp in his truck. In short order the tow strap was hooked up, and we were pulled to the safety of the hard packed dirt. Once again I thanked him for his help and slipped him a ten-dollar bill in appreciation.

It was almost dark now, but a warm breeze was blowing softly. Shaking the sand from my hair and clothes, I reflected that we had been in Baja for only a few hours and already there had been plenty of adventure—maybe even a little bit too much adventure.

Getting stuck in the sand proved to be a valuable lesson for me to learn early in the trip. By learning the truck's limitations, I was able to keep out of trouble and avoid similar predicaments throughout our trip when there wasn't anyone around to help pull us out. Had I waited to learn this lesson later on when we were miles and miles away from help, things might have turned out much differently.

Kat was quiet and didn't say much as we prepared for our first night in Baja. She could have said a number of things, but it wasn't necessary. After doing something that foolish, nothing really needs to be said. Even still, Kat is pretty forgiving and I could tell she wouldn't stay mad for long.

We bedded down in the back of the truck and were finally able to relax after a stressful evening. Even after the night's snafu, I looked around at my surroundings and felt a contented smile forming on my lips. What an awesome day! We watched a full moon rise up over the water and drifted off to sleep with moonbeams in our eyes.

Day 2

The sky was a clear thin blue color when we awoke, and the sun was just appearing over the horizon. As we sat up in our sleeping bags we could see that the tide had come in overnight so the water was much closer. Getting out of our bed in the back of the truck, the sand was cool as it squished between my toes. A chill hung in the air, and I was excited for the sun to rise higher in the sky and begin to warm things up.

We ate a quick breakfast of instant oatmeal and decided to walk down to the water. I ruefully glanced over at the large depression and tire tracks on the beach and shook my head. Kat smiled but didn't rub it in too much. Even with the tide in there was still a strip of muddy tidal flat that prevented me from reaching the water's edge. I nearly lost a flip-flop trying to cross the mud and had to retreat with mud up to my knees. Some people just don't learn.

Excited to get on the road, we walked back to camp and got ready to leave. We headed out to the main highway and turned toward San Felipe. The truck didn't seem to suffer any ill effects from its ordeal in the sand, so we crossed our fingers and pushed on. It was pretty early when we rolled into San Felipe, and the town was still asleep. Since most of the shops were closed, we decided to head to the waterfront to walk around.

San Felipe is a colorful little town that serves as a party destination for those who cross the border from Arizona. It is a much smaller town than Ensenada and sees fewer tourists. Instead of luxury beach resorts and places for cruise ships to dock, San Felipe is known for its abundant RV parks and local fishing fleet. The local economy is driven by tourist dollars, but the place has managed to retain much of its small-town charm.

San Felipe has a wonderful sidewalk promenade called the malecón, which flanks a long curved beach. This avenue is lined with curio shops and hole-in–the-wall restaurants. A flotilla of brightly colored fishing boats sits on the beach, their hulls painted with brilliant colors such as turquoise, fire engine red, and sky blue. Most lie at jaunty angles in the sand, waiting for the tide to come in.

Fishermen linger on the boardwalk ready to pounce on any unsuspecting tourist walking by their boat with the goal of convincing them that they should go out fishing. Since it was still early and we were some of the only tourists on the malecón, we were prime candidates for the fishermen's attention. The fishermen were a persistent bunch, eager to entice us to charter their boat for the day.

There are many cultural differences between Americans and Mexicans that we noticed as soon as we crossed the border. One of the most obvious differences, which we were confronted with as soon as we entered Tijuana, is the manner in which business is conducted in tourist areas. There are an abundance of people who want your business, and money, of course, and waste no time in letting you know so.

Merchants, restaurant owners, vendors, and even fishermen have no problem engaging you in conversation to convince you of the merits of their particular wares or services. There is no stigma or embarrassment in yelling, talking, chatting, and convincing you that they have the best item at the best price— even after you have said you aren't interested. You have to be quick on your feet with this verbal jousting, or you will find yourself on a full-day fishing charter that you didn't know you wanted to take. It's sometimes hard to say no, and I'm not too proud to admit that their sales techniques overpowered my ability to say no several times during the trip.

After walking up and down the malecón and convincing several fishermen that we really didn't want to go fishing on their boats, we headed back to the truck. Our next stop was the Virgin of Guadalupe Shrine.

The Virgin of Guadalupe is the patron saint of the town, and a shrine has been erected in her honor. This shrine is located on a tall hill that overlooks the town and is reached by climbing over one hundred and twenty steps. We could see the monument from the malecón and decided to check it out. We drove a few blocks past the shipyard, feeling our way through the empty streets, until we reached the base of the staircase.

We parked the truck next to a rotting pile of garbage and got out to climb to the top of the hill. The shrine consisted of a small statue enclosed in a dingy concrete hut with steel bars to protect it from vandalism. Empty beer bottles and broken glass littered the area, and the unmistakable stench of urine was pervasive. However, what the shrine lacked in magnificence, the view more than compensated for.

From up on top of the hill we could see the whole town of San Felipe laid out before us. We snapped several pictures and watched for a few minutes as the sleepy town started to awake. We could see the fishermen on the beach readying their boats and the merchants opening their front doors and setting up their displays. We tromped back down the stairs to the truck and made one final stop at the Pemex station to fill up with fuel before leaving town.

Back on Highway 3 we headed south toward the little town of Puertocitos. I was especially excited for this next stretch of the trip. Highway 3 essentially ends in San Felipe, and only a much smaller secondary road continues southward. Tourists seldom travel the next hundred miles due to rough roads and lack of accommodations.

The paved road ends about fifteen miles south of San Felipe. From this point on the road deteriorates into a narrow, rocky dirt road that parallels the Sea of Cortez. This road follows the coastline for about seventy miles and then turns eastward and eventually links back up with Highway 1. Several of the guidebooks recommended four-wheel drive for this part, but I was pretty sure the truck could handle it. I would be lying, however, if I said I wasn't a little nervous after the sand incident the night before.

The secondary road past San Felipe started off in good condition with smooth, even pavement, and as the miles passed by we started to joke that maybe the guidebooks were confused and it was now paved all the way. Of course not five minutes later the road's condition quickly changed. The potholes that Mexican roads are infamous for began to dot the highway. Minutes later the potholes began to overpower the crumbling asphalt, and eventually the pavement disappeared completely. I guess the guidebooks had it right after all.

It was slow going from then on as the road deteriorated into an uneven dusty dirt track. Kat struggled to read the map as we bounced along but soon reported that we were getting close to Valle de los Gigantes.

We had been looking forward to visiting the Valle de los Gigantes, which translates into Valley of the Giants. This is an area that has a dense concentration of huge cardón cactuses and has been turned into a nature preserve of sorts. We were alerted to the entrance of the park by a faded hand-painted sign that looked like it had seen better days.

Turning off the main road, we proceeded to a gate with an ancient trailer home parked nearby. A windmill turned lazily in the light breeze and water gurgled into a watering trough. Several skinny cows stared languidly at us while their tails swayed back and forth swatting at the swarms of black files that hovered around them. The park's caretaker stepped out of the shade of the trailer and walked over and greeted us with a smile and a "Buenos Días." We paid the five dollar admission fee and were handed a grainy Xeroxed map with a brief explanation of the history of the Valle de los Gigantes on the backside. He mentioned that we were the only visitors so far that day, and we would have to watch for cattle on the road. "Does the road have any sandy spots?" I asked as casually as possible. He looked our truck up and down and replied that we should have no trouble. He unlocked the gate, and I pretended that I wasn't concerned about the sand either as we rolled over the cattle guard and down the suspiciously sandy road.

The cardón cactus is a monstrous plant that can grow to over thirty feet in height. It has thick olive colored trunks that sprout from the ground and grow close together, reaching for the sky. Each trunk is covered in rows of sharp white quills, and tennis-ball-sized flower pods sprout near the tips of the trunks. Their sheer size is absolutely staggering.

The valley floor was thick with cactuses, and the dirt road weaved in and out of large stands of them. It was amazing to consider that such a massive plant could survive in such a dry climate and barren soil. The brochure stated that not only were the cactuses huge but very old as well. Some of the larger ones dated back over two thousand years. This variety of cactus is the Giant Sequoia of the desert and inspires similar feelings of grandeur. While marveling at their immense size, we had a picnic lunch and enjoyed being among such magnificent flora. I made sure to park the truck on a patch of firm soil and was relieved that we hadn't encountered too many deep sandy areas on the way in.

After lunch we decided it was time to press on and made our way back out to the main road.

The road rose and plunged as it clung to the coastal cliffs. On the one side we were flanked by the shoreline and on the other by rugged desert mountains. The Sea of Cortez had a steely blue color, and the surf crashed onto beaches of cobblestones. There were miles and miles of pristine beaches, unmarred by any sort of human development. We had plenty of time to admire the beaches since I had to drive slowly, weaving my way through the rocks that were strewn across the road.

It took us the next two hours to cover thirty miles of uninhabited coastline until we reached the tiny fishing village of Puertocitos. It is actually kind of an exaggeration to call it a village. Puertocitos consists of a handful of run-down cinderblock houses with an unfinished Pemex gas station on the far end. It was a good thing that our spare gas cans were full, because we still had many miles to cover before returning to civilization. The ragtag settlement soon disappeared in the rear view mirror as we pressed onward.

Washboard roads: the mere mention of them brings terror into the heart of anyone who has spent any amount of time driving them. The constant jarring they produce not only deadens the rear end but also the mind. Driving on these roads is akin to Chinese water torture. At first the vibrations and bumps are tolerable, but soon you find yourself wondering if it will ever stop.

To take my mind off the increasingly annoying jostling, I glanced over at the speedometer and realized that at the current pace, there would be at least six more hours of this incessant jarring to endure before reaching camp. As much as I wanted the bumping to end, I knew that to reach camp I would have to suck it up and keep going, no matter how much I just wanted to sit still without all my insides bouncing around. (Yes, they are that much fun.)

Washboard roads derive their name from the texture of the road, which consists of millions of earthen grooves, several inches deep, that run perpendicular to the direction you are traveling. How they come to be is a mystery to me, but I think it must be a form of soil erosion. It seems that some types of soil are more resistant to developing a washboard surface, because once in a great while we would find a dirt road without any washboard.

Whatever the cause, washboard roads seem to be in every corner of Baja. They are the bane of backcountry travel and certainly limit the amount of dirt road driving that one can endure. A few hours spent on a bad washboard road can feel like an eternity. Unfortunately, washboard roads have to be endured if one is to leave the beaten path and see Baja's backcountry.

There are two schools of thought on the proper way to deal with washboard roads. The first method is to take it very slow, driving only about 4 mph, and to deal with the slow but less bumpy ride. Theoretically this spares your vehicle from rattling itself to death and saves your rear end. The second manner to negotiate such a road is to drive closer to 40 mph and skim over the top of the bumps, thus lessening the jarring effect, but by doing so sacrificing most of your ability to steer or brake effectively. As you can see, both methods have their respective strong points and drawbacks.

Since Baja is chock full of washboard roads, we had plenty of time to try both methods. Neither one is perfect, and no matter how you drive washboard roads they are hard on your vehicle, rear end, and mental health. After hours and hours of experimentation, we decided that you have to use both the fast and slow method in order to survive the endless miles of washboard roads that crisscross Baja.

As we slowly crept over the washboard, we soon realized why we had seen so little traffic on the road. This road was not exactly made for the casual tourist with its steep grades, tight turns, and washboard surface. There also weren't a lot of creature comforts along the way — no taco stands, no hotels, no houses, no nothing.

For many hours we didn't even see any other vehicles on the road, or any people for that matter. Then a pack of dune buggies roared up behind us in a cloud of dust. With a wave of hello and goodbye they sped around us and off into the distance. They definitely prescribed to the over 40 mph theory of travel. Kat and I exchanged knowing glances and hoped that the fact that we had only seen off-road type vehicles all day didn't spell trouble for us.

It was amazing to find ourselves in such a remote location so quickly. Just yesterday we were battling our way through southern California's infamous traffic jams, surrounded by miles of urban sprawl in every direction. Suddenly today we were out on a lonely dirt road overlooking the tranquil waters of the Sea of Cortez, miles from anywhere. Even though we were only a few hundred miles south of the border, it already felt like we were a world away.

We stopped frequently to enjoy the vistas and stretch our legs. Around noon we found a nice beach where we could stop and have a picnic lunch.   After lunch Kat got busy collecting shells while I had a good time lying on the rocks watching the pelicans play in the waves. I dipped a toe in the water and shivered — it was still pretty chilly.

Somehow someone dared someone to jump in, and before we knew it clothes lay strewn about on the rocks, and we were screaming and splashing each other as we played in the water. We didn't last too long in the chilly water and soon lay on the warm rocks to let the sun dry our skin. Slightly damp and sticky with salt, we walked barefoot back to the truck.

The afternoon grew long and shadows began to fall across the valleys. It was time to start thinking about looking for a spot to camp. Due to the cliffs and rugged coastline, camping spots were somewhat limited. We found a few prime camping spots in secluded coves, but other groups were already using them. In the end we decided to press on to Bahía San Luis Gonzaga where there were several campgrounds.

We found a nice campground area on the northern end of Bahía San Luis Gonzaga and decided to call it a day. It had taken us the better part of the day to travel only sixty-five miles, and we were tired and ready to get out of the car.

The camp we picked was situated in a protected cove surrounded by tall cliffs on three sides. To get to the camping area it was necessary to drive up a steep dirt road that went through a cleft in one of the cliffs, and subsequently the beach was very private and secluded. The beach was covered with marble sized pebbles and lots of broken shells. Careful to avoid soft sand, I backed the truck up to the beach, and we began to unload the Tupperwares and set up camp.

I was excited to use the small charcoal BBQ that I had bought especially for the trip. Soon steaks were sizzling over the coals as we watched the sun set over the cliffs. As the sun sank lower and lower, a deep shadow crept down the beach until it covered our camp. Once again we found ourselves camping alone. While munching on T-bones we surveyed the cove and anticipated putting the kayak on the water in the morning.

Darkness fell and we lay in the back of the truck watching the tide come in. It had been a long bone-jarring day on the road, but we had been rewarded with some beautiful vistas and absolute solitude. The stars sparkled overhead, and we fell asleep with a gentle ocean breeze blowing across the beach.

The sky was streaked with windblown clouds, and the sun was just starting to make its first appearance over the tall cliffs that surrounded us. Blinking the sleep from my eyes, I glanced around and remembered where we were. I rolled out of my sleeping bag with a tingle of anticipation for what the day might bring.

Slowly awakening, I sat in my folding camp chair and looked out over the water. Kat soon got up and we started on breakfast. We mixed boiling water with our instant oatmeal packets and soon devoured them.

It was time for our maiden voyage out onto the Sea of Cortez. Kat and I had used our kayak many times in the lake near our house, but this was the first time we had attempted to use it in the ocean. The gentle waves lapping up onto the beach and the glassy rolling swell on the horizon looked forgiving, and we figured that this spot was good as any to give the kayak a test drive in the open ocean.

After a tipsy start, we launched into the surf and made our way out past the small breakers where the water was smooth and crystal clear. The air was cool, but the morning sun was starting to burn off the chill. It felt good to be out on the water.

As we paddled out around the point of the cove and into the rolling swell, a loud snort sounded behind us, and we turned quickly to see a large sea lion dive beneath the surface. He resurfaced about fifteen feet away from us, and we circled around for a closer look. He seemed to be as curious about us as we were about him, and he allowed us to get quite close. After

examining us for a minute he blinked and then raised a rubbery flipper, waving to us as he rolled onto his side and slipped beneath the shimmering surface of the water.

Paddling south along the shoreline, we entered an expansive bay that was dotted with small fish camps and houses. According to the map the bay is called Bahía San Luis Gonzaga, and it is protected from the open ocean by a rocky island about half a mile off shore. The island becomes a peninsula at low tide when a long narrow sandbar emerges and connects it with the mainland.

The revving of an outboard motor at the far end of the bay shattered the silence, and we noticed several groups of people on shore. Paddling deeper into the bay, we began to explore the island's protected shore and noticed fishing nets anchored to the bottom near the sandbar. The nets were hundreds of feet long and paralleled the coast. Paddling over to get a closer look, we could see the shimmer of fish entangled in the nets far below the surface. Still feeling a little awkward and unbalanced in the kayak, we didn't stay long looking at the nets for fear of tipping over and meeting the same fate as the fish below us.

The ocean floor grew shallow as we paddled farther into the bay, and soon we could see the sandy bottom. Schools of small silver fish were visible as they darted to and fro only inches beneath our kayak. The water was much warmer here in the shallow lagoon and was flat as glass. The lagoon was only a foot or two at the deepest, and we spotted several stingrays in the shallows. Once the rays sensed our presence they disappeared in a flurry of sand as they made a hasty retreat. After exploring the bay for an hour or two, we turned back and headed for camp.

Back in our private cove we beached the kayak and broke out the snorkeling gear. Kat and I swam out near the rocky point and chased the fish around for a while. The fish were plentiful, but the chilly water soon made us retreat.

Back on the road, washboard greeted us right away, and Kat was already looking at the map to calculate how many more miles we would have to endure. We guestimated that we still had at least thirty miles to go before reaching Highway 1.

The road continued south along the shoreline of Bahía San Luis Gonzaga, and we could see where we had paddled earlier that morning. Once we passed the bay, the road veered away from the coast and made a gentle turn westward toward Highway 1. The road leveled out and was fairly straight, giving me a chance to really test the 40 mph rule. Kat may disagree with me on this point, but I felt that it was quite exhilarating to travel on a dirt road at speeds in excess of 60 mph.

After hitting a few unexpected dips and feeling all four tires leave the road, Kat had to remind me that even though I felt like I was driving the Baja 1000, I wasn't, and that the truck wasn't designed to take such abuse. I could see that she had a valid point, so I tried to tone it down and keep all four wheels on the ground from that point on.

We approached Highway 1 with a sense of relief. Although we were dusty and well shaken, we were glad we went on this side trip. It hadn't been comfortable driving all those miles of washboard, but seeing the wild and rugged coastline of the Sea of Cortez was well worth it. We were stoked to have made it through without incident—it would have been devastating to have had to turn around and backtrack our way to Highway 3 due to impassible roads. We turned onto Highway 1 with a much greater appreciation for smooth pavement. The plan was to head south toward our next stopping point: Bahía de Los Angeles.

Highway 1 is the main artery that travels the length of the Baja peninsula. It was completed in 1973 and has made the lower part of peninsula much more accessible. The completion of Highway 1 was crucial to Baja's development. Prior to its completion, many parts of southern and central Baja remained very remote, and large portions of the peninsula remained unexplored and uninhabited.

Nowadays Highway 1 is a modern, paved, two-lane road—according to the Mexican Government. There is some truth to this statement, but don't let this lure you into a false sense of security. Highway 1 is not for the casual driver and demands respect. The lanes are narrow, only nine feet wide, with absolutely no shoulder on either side. Most of the highway is well maintained, but some sections of the highway are in disrepair and killer potholes lurk, waiting to jump out and eat the tire of the unsuspecting tourist. Guardrails are few and far between, and it is left to the responsibility of the driver to stay on the road.

Speed limit signs are posted, but they are also ignored by nearly all who drive the highway. According to one native we met, a simple rule of thumb when driving in Baja is to double whatever the sign says. In our experience most of the vehicles on the road seemed to follow this advice.

The one thing that Highway 1 does have going for it is the number of cars on the road. Even though it is the major throughway used to travel just about everywhere in Baja, the traffic is light, and it's not uncommon to go for ten or fifteen minutes without seeing another vehicle.

I first became acquainted with the phenomenon known as the Baja truck driver during the next few hours. These brave souls travel the highways in their 18-wheelers hauling freight to and fro, much like their counterparts up north, but that is where the similarities end. The truck drivers of Baja break the stereotype that is so ingrained in our minds of the slow, inconsiderate, and belligerent truck drivers we encounter north of the border. No, these truckers are something entirely different.

The semi trucks that we encountered on the roads of Baja appeared to be similar, at first glance, to the ones north of the border, albeit older and a bit more battered. But don't let their appearance fool you: the semis in Baja know how to move— fast, that is. The first thing you notice about the semis of Baja is that they haul ass. Period. Whether pulling up steep grades or winding down a mountain pass, you can pretty much count on the fact that the semi will be traveling faster than you are. I don't know how they manage to do it, but seeing is believing. I was amazed as I tried to hang with these big boys while weaving down the central range and soon found myself being left in the dust.

So after being blown away by the speeds at which they barrel along, you will start to notice how considerate these drivers are of others on the road. If by some chance you happen to be driving a race car and feel the need to pass one of these trucks, the trucker will help guide you around his rig by signaling his left turn blinker and waving his arm out the window when the coast is clear.

They are also a friendly bunch and will happily give you a wave and a honk of their air horn as they pass you . . . again. They have to be a skillful bunch of drivers as the conditions in which they drive are rigorous. The steep narrow roads have few guardrails, and the drop-offs are deadly. Occasionally there are roadside shrines to those who didn't quite make the corner.

It is a sight to behold when two semis pass each other going in opposite directions on the highway. The high rate of speed at which they travel, coupled with the narrowness of the lanes, requires precision driving. If all goes perfectly, with the lanes being as narrow as they are, there are only about eight to twelve inches in between the two as they pass. One can just imagine the catastrophic results should this go less than perfectly.

The highway was fast and felt smooth as butter after all that washboard, making the miles fly by quickly. It was a pleasant change of pace from the slow dirt roads of the previous few days. Our destination for that evening was the town of Bahía de Los Angeles. We would travel for less than an hour on Highway 1 and then turn eastward off the beaten path, heading back toward the Sea of Cortez.

The beauty of the road leading from Highway 1 to Bahía de Los Angeles is that it is a paved two-lane highway. Even still, Bahía de Los Angeles is a relatively small fishing town that doesn't see very much tourist activity due to its remoteness. The bay is ringed with several large islands and is known for its rich marine life. On the spur road leading to Bahía de Los Angeles we traveled for over an hour without seeing another car. We even had to slow at one point to let a herd of wild burros scatter from the roadway and flee into the desert scrub.

Cresting a hill, the view of the bay opened up to us. The deep blue water contrasted sharply with the muted browns of the desert shore. Several large islands, majestic and forlorn, shimmered in the afternoon sun. We immediately noticed the wind. Strong gusts rocked the truck, and there were visible whitecaps out in the bay. From our vantage point we could see that the road meandered down the desert plateau in sweeping S-curves until it met the water's edge.

The town of Bahía de Los Angeles consists of one main street that parallels the shore. The street is lined with small beach houses on one side and small restaurants and shops on the other. The main drag goes for maybe a mile and that's it. The wind kicked up huge dust clouds that blew through the town and whipped the bay white. Due to the hurricane strength wind, we decided to find lunch in town rather than try to put something together ourselves.

We picked a little diner by the name of Las Hamacas. It was slightly more upscale than we were used to with indoor seating, a waitress, and to top it off, a fresh tablecloth covering our table. The food was simple but tasty. Fried fish was the plate of the day. As we ate the wind continued to rattle the windows of the restaurant, and when I asked the waitress about the wind she confessed that although it was especially strong today, it was not uncommon for this time of year. She said that the windstorm had started several days ago and would most likely last a couple more before it subsided. So that pretty much meant no kayaking this afternoon out in the bay, which was okay because we were interested in visiting the sea turtle research center.

Only one of the guidebooks made mention of the sea turtle research center in Bahía de Los Angeles and the details, such as the exact location, were sketchy. Given the current weather situation we decided that this afternoon would be a good time to see if we could find it.

It took us awhile, but we were persistent and finally found it. The place was located down an unmarked dirt road on the edge of town that led to an abandoned RV Park. From there we had to enter the RV Park, drive to the far end, and follow another unmarked dirt road that finally led to the sea turtle center.

Calling this facility a research center was a bit of a stretch for those of us who are used to visiting such places as the Monterey Aquarium or Sea World. The sea turtle research center consisted of three concrete tanks, each about twelve feet wide, enclosed in a chain link fence with an information board outside. The information board gave a brief explanation of the project and said that tours would be provided upon request if you drove down the road to the manager's house and asked for José. Peering through the chain link fence we could see several turtles swimming around and figured what the heck, we'd like a tour.

So after asking at several houses for José, we finally found the right one. José was busy at the moment, but he sent his thirteen-year-old son Jorge to give us the tour. Jorge jumped in the back of the truck, and we drove back to the turtles.

Jorge opened up the cage and led us inside. He explained that these sea turtles make a migration from Japan to Baja each year, and due to declining numbers the turtles are caught and then allowed to grow to maturity in captivity. Once they are old enough, they are then released back into the wild. We got to look at the turtles up close, and Jorge pulled out a baby one for us to take a look at. We tried to take pictures of the turtles swimming around in the tanks, but the wind was so strong it rippled the surface of the water in the tank and distorted the image.

Jorge said that the project relied entirely on donations, and it was one of his daily chores to come over and feed the turtles. All in all it was a pretty cool place to visit, even if the name "sea turtle research center" made it sound a bit grander than it actually was. We slipped a hundred peso note into the donation box and gave Jorge a ride back to his house.

Our map showed several excellent camping spots north of town, and we decided to find a place to spend the night. Of course this involved traveling down the worst six miles of washboard road we had encountered yet. It was truly miserable stuff, but we were rewarded with some beautiful beach camping out on Punta Gringa.

Punta Gringa is a spit of land that juts out into the bay and forms its northern edge. We had the whole area to ourselves. There were numerous campsites, so we drove around and looked at each one of them till we found the best one. Certain that we had the best spot around, we backed the truck into our own private cove and set up camp about fifteen feet from the water's edge.

From camp we could see down the length of the bay and had a great view of a gigantic wind-blown cloud formation over the bay. We called it the "funnel cloud," but it's not what you would typically think of as a funnel. The cloud stretched the entire length of the bay, hovering like a huge spaceship waiting to invade. It was quite spectacular.

I tried to set up some wind protection with the tarp strung over the kayak rack, but the wind still whipped around us. Even though it was chilly with the wind blowing, we decided to try some snorkeling.

After sticking a toe in the water, we quickly decided that wetsuits would be required. Kat struggled to put her wetsuit on for several minutes until I looked over and could see that she was putting it on inside out. We laughed and laughed as I helped her yank it back off and then try to put in on right side out. It was still super tight, and it was a struggle to put it on even with me trying to help. We both thought the whole wetsuit fiasco was pretty funny.

The water was crystal clear but cold. It reminded me of the waters around the Channel Islands. So after some initial gasping and screaming about how cold it was, we put our heads under and took a look around. I instantly got a cold headache but persevered and soon forgot about it as I started to look around below me.

There weren't many fish around, but the rock formations and clear water made it enjoyable. The sharp contrast between the silence underwater and the wind howling on the surface made it especially fun. Kat found a new kind of starfish that we hadn't seen before. It was a deep purple color with almost twenty arms. After swimming around for an hour or so we were thoroughly chilled and decided to get out and make dinner. Hot soup warmed our tummies, and we set up our beds in the back of the truck.

Gusts of wind shook the truck, and we huddled in the back behind the tarp. I supplemented our windscreen by stacking Tupperwares and stuffing beach towels into the cracks. As the sun set I hoped that the wind might die down, but alas its fierce bursts continued to rock the truck.

Even though the night was young, we settled into our warm sleeping bags and read our books by headlamp. The windscreen shielded us for the most part, but it was unsettling to have the tarp flapping about and the truck shake every time a big gust hit us. After reading for a while, we turned off our headlamps and lay huddled together, watching the silver clouds sail across the dark sky before dozing off.

Map of Days 4, 5, and 6

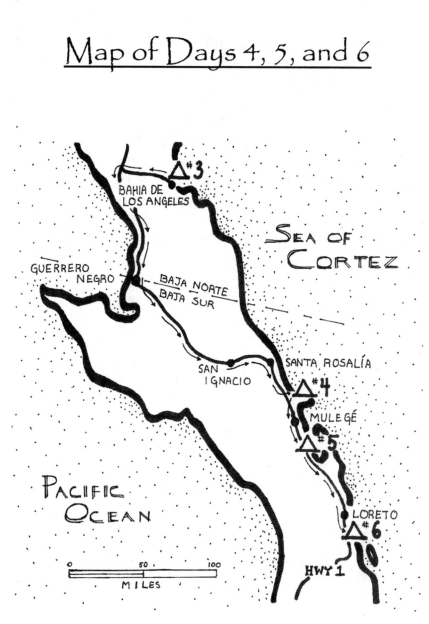

SEA OF CORTEZ

BAHIA DE LOS ANGELES

#3

GUERRERO NEGRO

BAJA NORTE
BAJA SUR

SAN IGNACIO

SANTA ROSALÍA

#4

MULEGÉ

#5

PACIFIC OCEAN

LORETO

#6

HWY 1

0   50   100
MILES

The truck was rocked and battered all night by the gale force bursts of wind. This constant barrage made for a restless night's sleep, and we awoke with the sun barely poking up over the horizon.

With the wind still howling, we decided to pack up camp and move along rather than try to wait it out. I was disappointed not to be able to kayak out in the bay, but I hoped that maybe we would return on our way back north and experience some better weather. Unfortunately, time didn't permit us to return to Bahía de Los Angeles, and the bay will have to be explored on another trip.

Our water supply was running low, so before we left town we decided to try to find some clean water to fill our jugs. We found a small grocery store in town that sold purified water and filled up. I also filled our sun shower for the first time and carefully laid it out in the back of the truck to absorb the warmth of the sun as we drove that day.

The sun shower is a large plastic water pouch that is clear on one side and black on the other with a short hose sticking out the bottom. You simply fill it up in the morning, let it sit in the sunlight for several hours, and then you have a hot shower that afternoon. This item was indispensable during our trip, and we ended up using it almost every evening once we set up camp. It wouldn't have been possible to camp for so many days in a row without the sun shower.

Heading out of town we looked over the map and realized that today would be a long day of driving. It was hundreds of miles before we would reach a nice camping spot. It was a fairly quick drive back to Highway 1, and we turned south toward Guerrero Negro.

Baja is a land of emptiness. There is no better way to describe it. The majority of Baja's 55,000 square miles is completely devoid of human development. This becomes very apparent while driving Highway 1. As you look out the window, the desert stretches on for hours at a time without interruption. Dry hills covered with scrubby desert plants and towering cardón cactuses are all you can see. This is not to say that the scenery is boring or all the same. Arroyos cut across the desert, and strange rock formations clutter the desert floor. Clumps of yucca sprout out of the dusty soil, and the occasional elephant tree is silhouetted on the ridgeline. The sheer vastness and loneliness of Baja's interior give it much of its beauty. It is a reminder of what much of southern California looked like and could still be if circumstances had turned out differently.

After passing through the empty desert for a few hours, we were able to glimpse the Pacific Ocean again as the highway swung toward the western side of the peninsula. The dark blue of the ocean was a pleasant change from the browns and muted greens of the desert, and we were excited to see signs of human civilization again.

Guerrero Negro is a very popular whale watching town during the winter months and can get quite busy in January and February, but during the off-season things slow considerably. Guerrero Negro is also an important town because of its location near the border between Baja Norte and Baja Sur. The Baja Peninsula is divided into two distinct states by the Mexican Government: Baja

California Norte and Baja California Sur. Guerrero Negro straddles this border and has a large military presence, along with an immigration checkpoint.

In general Baja has a large military presence. This was something that the guidebooks either glossed over or I intentionally ignored when planning the trip. Once you pass Ensenada, you can expect to pass through a military checkpoint every hundred miles or so.

These checkpoints consist of couple of sandbag bunkers on either side of the road, manned by several teenage soldiers in full combat fatigues carrying machine guns. As you near one of these checkpoints there are signs warning you to slow and prepare to have your vehicle searched.

As you slowly roll to a stop, a young solider will come up to your window and ask you where you are coming from, where you are going, what you are doing, and when you are returning. If the solider is inclined, he can have you step out of your car and then do a search. It is my understanding that they are looking for guns or drugs — the two big no-no's in Baja.

These checkpoints are everywhere. We even encountered military checkpoints on some of our travels on very remote back roads. At first these checkpoints were intimidating and a little frightening, but we soon grew accustomed to seeing two teenagers with machine guns in the road. All of the soldiers we encountered were friendly and courteous. Overall we were fortunate and had a pleasant experience while passing through the military checkpoints.

One of the first things that struck me while passing through our first military checkpoint was how young the soldiers looked. They were still in their late teens and probably most of them didn't even need to shave yet. Very few of them seemed to speak English, and I felt fortunate to be able to converse in Spanish with them. I think the checkpoints would have been much more intimidating if I hadn't been able to speak Spanish. It was rare that they searched our truck other than poking around at some of our camping stuff in the back.

It looked like hot, dusty, boring work checking cars all day, and I could tell that the soldiers were starved for real conversation. After asking the standard questions and realizing that this gringo (me) actually spoke Spanish, their faces brightened and they clustered around to ask about our trip and admire our camping gear. Most of the soldiers were interested in our quest to drive the whole length of the peninsula and asked additional questions about our trip. At most checkpoints I ended up talking for several minutes with the soldiers before passing through. They all got a kick out of the fact that Kat didn't speak any Spanish and couldn't understand what we were talking about.

By chatting with a soldier at one of the more remote checkpoints we encountered, I learned that in some of the more remote areas like the one we were passing through, the soldiers spend over a month at a time manning the checkpoint. They are dropped off with enough food and water to last the month and then left out there till the next unit comes to relieve them. He said that sometimes only one or two cars pass by each day and that it can get pretty boring.

Military duty in Baja certainly didn't look like much fun, but all the soldiers I spoke with agreed that the army provided one of the few ways to get out of their small villages and earn a living. The lack of employment opportunities in Baja is a real problem, and many of the young men have few options other than to stay in the family village and continue to live at a subsistence level.

Fifteen or twenty miles before we reached Guerrero Negro we encountered a large military checkpoint. This was a larger and more permanent looking setup than we had seen up to this point. There were several cinderblock buildings and many more soldiers than we had previously seen. As we slowed and waited our turn to be checked out, an officer came over to our window. He looked older than the other soldiers and was wearing a special uniform. It was obvious that he was in some sort of leadership position, and his interest in us made me a little nervous. He asked the standard questions in Spanish, which I promptly answered. He finished the conversation by asking, "Ehride?" "Qué?" I asked looking confused. "Ehride?" he repeated, but I still didn't understand what he was saying. He then pointed to four soldiers standing behind him and then pointed to the back of the truck. I realized he was saying "ride" in English and was asking if we could give these guys a lift into Guerrero Negro.

Not really knowing if this was a question or more of an order, I nodded the affirmative and the four soldiers jumped up into the back of the truck. Kat was a little nervous having four armed soldiers ride in the back, but I figured it was on our way and heck, they were already in the back of our truck, so off we went. They rode with us for about thirty minutes until we reached the military base in Guerrero Negro, and we dropped them off without incident. It really wasn't a big deal, but it was kinda crazy to be hauling around the Mexican army in the back of our truck. Kat felt much better after they departed and we were back on our own.

We decided to drive into town to see what Guerrero Negro had to offer. It is a dusty town that smells strongly of sea brine. A wide boulevard lined with short squat palm trees passes through the center of town. Boxy looking cement and cinderblock buildings are laid out in neat rows. Due to the lack of trees, lumber is scarce and almost all of the buildings in Baja are constructed of cement or cinderblocks.

We stopped briefly at a grocery store to buy a few food items. It certainly wasn't like the grocery store near our house and was an eye-opener for us both. The produce section was small and consisted mainly of wilted cabbage and a small selection of other vegetables, but it was the meat department that was the shocker. Refrigeration and cleanliness are certainly not as high a priority as they are here in the States. Swarms of flies hovered above the piles of meat as they sat out on the display counter. We both made a mental note to avoid buying meat while in Baja. We selected some handmade tortillas and picked out some fruit popsicles to cool us off.

While driving out of town we spotted a small Internet café on the other side of the street, flipped a quick U-turn, parked, and then when we got to the front door realized it was closed—Sunday. After being gone for four days we figured it would be a good idea to let our families know that we were alive and well and thoroughly enjoying our Baja adventure.

Instead of eating in town, we decided to have a roadside picnic several miles south of town. After lunch we pulled out the map again and were excited to notice that we were now on the back of the map. The main map that we used for our trip is the standard issue AAA map of Baja. Due to Baja's long narrow shape, Baja Norte is on the front side and Baja Sur is on the back. It was a major accomplishment and milestone for us to now be on the back of the map.

In just four days we were approaching the halfway point between the border and Cabo San Lucas. At least we were now on the same page as our goal. The next city we would reach would be San Ignacio. The guidebooks spoke highly of San Ignacio. They all described it as the first real desert oasis city that you will reach while traveling south. San Ignacio is acknowledged as a transition point where the geography and flavor of northern Baja begin to change to the more tropical feel of Baja Sur.

Cresting a rocky hill covered in scraggy desert flora, we caught our first glimpse of San Ignacio. The town is situated in a long narrow valley that is covered by date palms. The splash of green was a welcome sight after traveling through a sea of muted browns for the last few days.

San Ignacio is one of the oldest settlements in Baja, founded by Franciscan missionaries in 1728. These missionaries planted the palm groves and set up one of the largest missions on the peninsula. San Ignacio was one of the larger settlements in Baja but with the collapse of the mission system, it has faded into obscurity.

One of the main reasons that San Ignacio is so green and vibrant is the fact that it has major water source nearby. A wide river meanders through the palms and stands in stark contrast to the dry hills that surround the valley.

Turning off Highway 1, we descended farther into the valley toward the small village. The road is lined by tall date palms, and a narrow one-lane bridge crosses over the cool blue-green water leading toward the town. The river is atypical because it seeps out of the desert sand several miles outside of town, surfaces and flows above ground for a couple of miles, and then disappears back beneath the desert sand, making only that brief appearance. As we neared the town center, the smooth asphalt abruptly ended and knobby cobblestones took their place.

We soon found ourselves driving down an ancient cobblestone path leading to the main plaza. The town center follows the classic Latin American design: a square plaza with a shady tree-covered park in the center, surrounded by small shops, with the church on one side. The ancient mission church takes its place at the head of the park and presides over the plaza.

The plaza was nearly deserted with almost all of the shops closed on this sleepy Sunday afternoon. We parked and got out to wander around the plaza and church. Misión San Ignacio de Loyola was impressive in both appearance and age. It dates back several hundred years and was built under the direction of Jesuit missionaries in 1728. It was renovated by the Dominicans in 1786 and is one of the more elaborate mission churches in Baja. We poked our heads into the church's doorway, and through the cool dark gloom we could see the ancient wooden pews and muted colors of stained glass windows. All was quiet inside, and we could sense the history contained in the thick adobe walls.

Retreating from the church back out into the plaza, we took a quick stroll around the park to stretch our legs. There were several older gentlemen sitting in the park around a table, chatting and playing checkers. The air was cool under the trees, and we could hear the distant bray of a donkey. A vegetable merchant pushed his wooden cart across the plaza while two old women conversed in the open doorway of a tiny shop. Looking around the plaza, we noticed that ours was the only motorized vehicle in sight. It felt like we had entered a time warp and traveled back fifty, maybe even a hundred years, to a slower more simple way of life. Even though time had apparently slowed down in San Ignacio, we still had many more miles to cover, so we reluctantly packed back into the truck and drove out through the date palms to the highway.

Back on the highway I was ready to cover some ground, and I set the cruise control for 120 km/hr. My plan to make good time was quickly halted as we ran into the back of a long line of cars traveling very slowly on the highway. I figured there must be some sort of accident or road construction and slowed down and eased in behind the last vehicle.

After five or ten minutes of traveling at only a few miles per hour, I started to get impatient. "What could the holdup possibly be?" I asked while anxiously drumming my fingers on the steering wheel. I craned my neck out the window, trying to get a better view of what was impeding traffic. As we crested a small hill I could see a green pick up truck at the front of the line, about twenty cars ahead, holding up traffic. "What a jerk," I thought, "that guy needs to get off the road and let everyone around him." I was flabbergasted that cars weren't zipping around him, and I started to think about making an end run around them all.

Luckily, a few moments later the slow truck up in the front pulled off to the side of the road, and the line of cars followed him as he paralleled the highway. "What is going on?" Kat wondered out loud. At this point I was just glad to see the roadblock moving off to the side and was ready to give the truck a dirty look as we passed by. Picking up speed, we were soon able to get around the line of cars, and as we neared the green truck I noticed a casket in the bed—this was a funeral procession, Baja style.

Now it was my turn to feel like a jerk for being so impatient. We passed the makeshift hearse as it entered the small dusty cemetery near the side of the highway, and we soon left the funeral procession behind. "Wow, that was different," Kat commented, and we both sat silent for a minute or two. We were both impressed with the simplicity and matter of factness of the funeral procession.

At this point Highway 1 makes a turn toward the east and follows the coastline of the Sea of Cortez. The next town on the map was Santa Rosalía. Santa Rosalía is a rough and tumble working town. The guidebooks had very little to say about the place other than it had a strong French influence due to the French mining company that ran a large copper mine near town. The mine has long since closed, but the town still has a gritty industrial feel to it.

Pressed for time, we didn't stop and explore but drove through the outskirts while on Highway 1. Looking at the map, we selected a camping spot out near Punta Chivato. Punta Chivato is a point of land that forms the northern edge of Bahía Santa Inés. To reach this area we had to take yet another slow, bumpy, washboard road. It seemed that just about everywhere we had gone so far required a drive on a slow, bumpy, washboard road.

The guidebooks describe this as a remote area with lots of good primitive camping. Well, that may have been true at one time, but it's no longer the case. Unfortunately the area has been overrun by new and spacious beach homes, undoubtedly owned by rich Americans. As we drove out onto the peninsula, we hoped that the homes would soon start to fade away behind us, but to our disappointment they continued right out to the very point.

Discouraged after a long day of driving and not wanting to backtrack for over an hour on bad roads back out to the highway, we gritted our teeth and searched for the best spot to stay the night. We eventually found an area that was open for camping, but at least five other groups had found it before us and all of the better spots were taken.

To make matters worse, to get out close to the water we would have to drive across a seventy-five-foot expanse of soft beach sand. Still smarting from my last run-in with beach sand, I didn't dare try to cross it. After saying quite a few bad words, I finally accepted the fact that no matter how much I wanted to drive out onto the beach, the truck would have to stay on this side of the sand. Fuming and irritated, I selected a less than desirable spot on firmer ground and we set up camp.

We were both a little cranky from last night's sleep in the wind, the long drive, billions of beach houses, and others intruding on "our" camping spot. Kat tried to look at the bright side, but I wasn't having any of it. We ate a quick dinner while the sun was setting and then retired early for bed.

The rhythmic crash of the surf soothed our nerves as we lay in our sleeping bags, and gradually, as I began to relax, things didn't seem quite so bad. As we drifted off to sleep, a full orange moon crept up over the water and softly illuminated the waves breaking on shore.

Day 5

Dawn greeted us as we stirred in our sleeping bags. Poking my head out, I was greeted with a clear blue sky and the squawk of sea gulls on the beach. In the morning light our camping spot didn't seem nearly so bad. Waves crashed on the beach only yards away, and the water looked clean and inviting. The frustrations of the previous night were quickly forgotten as we got ready to enjoy a morning of kayaking and snorkeling.

Before readying the kayak and other gear, we decided to go for a quick stroll down the beach to get our blood moving. After crossing the dunes, we discovered that the beach was littered with all kinds of seashells—millions of them—stretching from one end of the beach to the other. Of course this meant that we would have to examine just about every single one of them and then collect only the best ones for Kat's growing shell collection. I don't think I have ever seen quite so many seashells on one beach before. Eventually I had to pull Kat away with the promise that we could do some more collecting after kayaking around a bit.

We carried the kayak over the scrubby dunes and waded out into the water to launch it. The water was much warmer than it had been previously and hinted that we would soon be in the tropics. Since our kayak is a double, Kat climbed into the front, and I waited for a lull to push us out. A break in the waves appeared, and I gave the kayak a big push while trying to hop into my seat in the back, nearly upsetting it. It was pretty standard for us to nearly tip over each time we tried to launch. Toward the end of the trip we got more proficient, but it was always kind of touch and go when we first launched out through the surf.

Having made a successful launch, we dug in our paddles and headed out around the point. Staying close to the shore, we noticed that the rocks were alive with small red crabs. Setting the paddles across our laps, we paused and tried to get as close as possible to the rocks to watch the crabs scamper around. As the swell pushed us closer and closer, we had to do some quick paddling to avoid washing up onto the rocks.

We explored several small coves and decided to beach the kayak in one of them and snorkel around. There were quite a few fish swimming around, and we saw a couple of small jellyfish. Not knowing the correct scientific names of the marine life, we made up names for the different fish we saw, such as stripeys, clown fish, and arrow fish. We regretted not having a fish identification card to help us learn the proper names. Even though we couldn't identify the fish by their proper names, we were able to take their pictures with our disposable waterproof camera while snorkeling. It was fun to chase after a fish in hopes of getting a good close-up picture.

After swimming around for an hour or so we started to get hungry, so we paddled back. We beached the kayak and spent another hour or two on the beach collecting seashells before moseying back to camp.

It was, once again, time for the daily ritual of packing up. By now we had a system worked out to load everything back into the truck. Kat took care of loading up the kitchen Tupperware and getting out the food we would need for lunch, while I usually took care of packing up the snorkel stuff. Together we had to lift the kayak up onto the rack and slide it into place. We then had to stuff our sleeping bags, roll our Paco pads, and gather up loose clothing. The water jugs and Jerry cans of gasoline had to be strapped into place in the bed of the truck, and the BBQ had to be secured. All in all it took about twenty minutes for us to break camp and get back on the road.

After five days on the road, we had now settled into a comfortable travel routine of waking up early with the sun, kayaking or exploring around camp in the morning, packing up, and then driving a few hours to our next camping location. We tried to limit our driving time to around four or five hours a day so that we could pull into camp around midafternoon and relax, swim, kayak, or snorkel the afternoon away. We usually cooked a simple dinner and watched the sun set over the water. Every evening after dinner as the sun was setting, I would sit in my folding camp chair and record our day's events in the Baja journal. As it got dark we would get sleepy and then talk or read our books in the moonlight before falling asleep. This simple, natural way of life — Baja style — was such a breath of fresh air in comparison to our hectic schedules up north.

Rattling along past all of the beach houses, we shook our fists in their direction and continued on our way back toward Highway 1. We had a short day of driving planned to make up for yesterday's six hours in the car. Our next stop would be the town of Mulegé, which was only about twenty-five miles down the road.

Mulegé is similar to San Ignacio in its desert oasis appearance but is a much larger town. Founded in 1705 by the Jesuits, the town was subsequently destroyed in 1770 by a tropical storm. The town was rebuilt but remained a small settlement until the mid 1800s. The construction of Highway 1 transformed Mulegé from a mainly agricultural economy to almost completely dependent on tourism. Today Mulegé marks the gateway to Bahía Concepcion and all its outdoor attractions.

Mulegé is known for its narrow one-way streets and confusing twists and turns. With this in mind, we decided to do most of our exploring on foot and found a shady spot to park the truck. As we walked down the twisty streets and a saw how narrow they actually were, we were glad to be on foot instead of trying to drive.

In town we found an Internet café and were able to send off a few emails to our family to assure them that we were still alive and well. Ironically the connection was much faster than our own dial-up connection back at home. Of all the bargains to be found in Baja, Internet cafés have to be among the best. It cost us only about ten pesos to use the Internet for about an hour, which translates into less than one dollar an hour. After sending off our emails, we continued to walk around and see what else Mulegé had to offer.

While walking we passed a fire station, which I had to stop and check out. The shiny red fire engine was parked under an open awning with a tin roof. Next to the awning stood a small shed. The faded red sign on the door read "Bomberos." I knocked, but no one was home. Walking over to the engine, I could see "City of San Luis Obispo" painted on the side. Many fire departments in California send their older fire trucks and equipment down to Baja so that volunteer departments, such as the one in Mulegé, have equipment to use.

A little farther down the street we ran into the post office. Curious, we poked our heads inside. The interior was cool and dimly lit, and it took a few seconds for our eyes to adjust. Rows of small wooden cubbies lined the walls, and our footsteps echoed off the tile floor. Behind a tall counter the postmaster was sorting mail, and watching him gave us the idea that we should try to send home a postcard. Of course, the actual post office only sold stamps and didn't have any postcards. We had to leave the post office and walk a little farther down the street until we found a shop that sold postcards. We purchased a few and returned to the post office to mail them off. We both wondered how long it would take for them to reach their destinations. We dropped them into the mailbox and headed back out into the bright sunny morning. Walking back to the truck, we decided to drive across town to check out the mission church.

The mission chapel was built in 1754 and is still in use today. Its construction is unusual because of the round river rocks that were used to construct the thick outer walls, instead of the more traditional adobe bricks. The chapel was built on a rise overlooking the river that flows through Mulegé. There is a small hill next to the chapel with a stone staircase that leads to a lookout point at the top. The view of the river and palm covered valley floor was great, and we snapped a few pictures before leaving.

After seeing the mission we were ready for lunch. We found a fun roadside taco stand in town and ordered a batch of fish tacos. The tacos were excellent, and we polished off almost a dozen of them. After munching down the tacos we paid our bill of one hundred pesos, about ten dollars, and split.

Many people will warn you to stay away from roadside taco stands and to be careful about what you eat while in Baja. I will agree that there may be some wisdom to this advice, but if you follow it you will be missing out on the true Baja experience. One of our favorite things in Baja was all the wonderful food we ate along the way. We tried to use prudence when selecting where we would eat, but with our budget constraints we were generally eating with the locals. It may be more of the exception than the rule, but we never got sick from anything we ate during the trip.

In town I had inquired about where I could purchase some fresh fish to grill that evening. I was given directions to a fisherman's house and was told that he would probably sell me some fish. The directions went something like this: head south out of town about three kilometers; after the second set of speed bumps look for the telephone wires that cross the road; turn right down a small dirt road, and it's the third house on the right. I had really been hankering to grill some fresh fish for several nights now, so I decided we would give it a try.

The directions turned out to be pretty good, and we found the house on the first try. I parked the truck and got out to knock on the door. An older looking señora opened the door and looked surprised to find a gringo standing in front of her. I explained that I had been directed to her house and was looking to buy some fish. Regaining her composure she nodded and asked, "How much do you want?" Now it was my turn to be puzzled—how much fish *did* I want? I wasn't sure what sort of measurement was used when buying fish from a fisherman's grandmother: two fish, a few pounds, three tails worth? Noting my pensive look, she helped by suggesting half a kilo. Not really knowing how much that was, I decided that I'd better take a full kilo. "Déme un kilo." She shut the door and soon returned with a large plastic bag full of fresh fish fillets. I was relieved that she didn't bring me out a whole fish, because I'm not really sure that I would have known what to do with it. Handing over a few bills, I took the bag of fish and concluded with a "Muchas gracias."

It was pretty obvious that I was new to the fish buying game, and it's possible that I got taken advantage of, but I didn't really care. I happily paid the price that she quoted and returned to the truck holding my prize out in front of me to show Kat. I was mainly just excited to have found the right house and to now have some fish to cook up for dinner.

Highway 1 below Mulegé follows the coastline closely and has some spectacular views of the Sea of Cortez. Barren mountains rise steeply from the water, and the highway clings to their sides as best it can. Sheer drop-offs await the careless driver around every turn, and I had to limit my looking around and pay close attention to the road.

While driving around a particularly sharp hairpin turn, the panoramic view of Bahía Concepción opened up before us. Its brilliant tropical blue waters make a striking contrast against the rugged tan mountains that enclose it from the Sea of Cortez. Bahía Concepción is a long narrow bay—only a few miles wide but almost thirty miles long. Its sheltered waters are dotted with small rocky islands and the occasional fishing boat. The bay is known for its world-class kayaking and is a sport fisherman's paradise.

Even though it was still early, just after lunch, our minds were instantly made up that we would be camping along the shores of Bahía Concepción that evening. There were about five different campgrounds to pick from, and with it being early we decided to keep driving along the bay and find the best one. After checking them all out, we came back to Playa Coco and set up camp.

To sum it up in two words: tropical paradise. The campground stretched along a ribbon of white beach that was sheltered in a protected cove. Each campsite had its own palapa, a shade hut thatched with palm fronds, that was only few feet away from the clearest blue water you have ever seen. The icing on the cake was that we had the place to ourselves with only one other group camping down at the far end of the beach.

The temperature outside was a balmy eighty degrees, and a cool breeze rustled the dried palm fronds of our palapa. What looked like white sand from afar actually turned out to be millions of small white fragments of broken seashells. The coarse texture felt good underneath my bare feet as I stepped out onto the beach.

Our driving clothes were quickly replaced with swimsuits, and we tested out the water. It was like diving into warm bathwater. We donned snorkels and swam out from the beach toward the reef. It turns out that what we had thought was a reef was actually only a thick forest of seaweed. Subsequently there weren't as many fish around as we had hoped. Nonplussed, we chased around what fish there were and then swam back to the beach and just lay out, absorbing the sun's rays.

It was so nice to take a break from the driving and relax in the sun. As the afternoon wore on the wind picked up, so we broke out the kites and flew them for a while. It was truly amazing to think that we had reached this tropical destination simply by getting in our car several days earlier and pointing south.

A beat-up white minivan pulled up to our camp and two guys hopped out. I figured that they were the camp hosts and had come by to collect their fee. I meandered over and greeted them with a "Buenas Tardes" and my wallet in hand. We exchanged pleasantries, and I hoped that by being friendly they would cut me a break on the camping fee. Before I knew it the van's sliding door was opened and I was being offered T-shirts, bracelets, hats, and all sorts of other trinkets. I was blindsided with my wallet in hand, and I knew that it was futile to try to resist their persuasive sales pitches. These guys wouldn't take no for an answer, and with my wallet in my hand it would be pretty hard to convince them that I didn't have any money. Admitting defeat, I decided to buy the least expensive thing these guys had to offer. The real kicker was that I knew that when the real camp host came by I would have to pay him too.

Kat wandered over from under the shade of the palapa to see what was going on and right away sized up the situation correctly. These guys weren't going to leave until we bought something. It was just a matter of trying to find something that we liked and wasn't too expensive. I ended up getting a T-shirt with a map of Baja on the front, and Kat selected a coral necklace. Two hundred pesos richer, the minivan sped off down the beach looking for the next unsuspecting gringo.

Shaking my head at being snookered, we both walked back to the beach and examined our new souvenirs. While Kat napped on a beach towel, I decided to take the kayak out myself and check out the island that was a few bays down. It was a tough paddle with the wind kicking up, but I was rewarded when I reached the island and noticed that due to the water's clarity, I could see large schools of fish swimming beneath me.

The island was not much more than a guano-covered rock with several cactuses protruding from its crown, but the water around the island was teeming with sea life. As the swell grew larger with the increasingly strong wind, I decided that it would be prudent to head back to shore before it got really rough. The wind was blowing towards the shore, so it was an easy paddle as I rode the swell back to camp.

Kat was still hanging out on the beach when I returned. We flew the kites again, swam, and relaxed the rest of the afternoon away. I was excited as dinnertime approached and started my charcoals in anticipation of grilling the fish. When the coals got good and hot, I tossed the fish on the grill, shook on a little seasoning salt, and closed the lid. Ten minutes later I flipped them over, and soon we were eating some very tasty fish steaks — hot off the grill. I gave myself a pat on the back for having the foresight to buy the little BBQ a few weeks earlier. My eight-dollar investment in this small charcoal BBQ was certainly paying big dividends.

As the shadows lengthened, the flies began to appear. They were small, persistent, and numerous. We had noticed flies in several of our other camps, but this beach had quite a few more. They were especially bad as I tried to write in the journal. Hordes of them flew around my face and attacked my eyes. People seldom talk about the bugs when they expound upon the beauties of nature, but in my experience it is almost impossible to be out in the wild without coming into contact with a bunch of bothersome insects. (And yes, I'm aware they play an important part in the ecosystem, blah, blah, blah. . . . I still don't like them.) Unfortunately, bugs are just part of the experience and nothing can be done about them.

Clear small breakers lapped at the crushed shell beach as we sat in our folding camp chairs watching the sun set. Prior to leaving I had purchased John Steinbeck's *Log from the Sea of Cortez* to read during the trip. He is one of my favorite authors, but I hadn't read this particular book before and thought it might be fun to read while in Baja.

Tonight seemed like the perfect night to start it, and Kat thought it would be fun to read it out loud together. We read to each other for about an hour, enjoying the view and the fine literature. I was drawn in right from the beginning and knew that this would be a great read. Our plan for reading the book together deteriorated quickly as I cheated and started reading on my own while Kat took a shower.

Reading from this book in the evenings by headlamp turned out to be one the highlights of the trip for me. It was cool to be able to have similar experiences and visit many of the same places that Steinbeck mentions in his book. I discovered that we both felt the same sense of awe at Baja's raw beauty. I found myself looking forward to the time after dinner when I could sit in my camp chair with my headlamp and read more.

As it grew darker, we became more aware of the highway noise. The rumble of the trucks was quite loud as they zoomed past us in the darkness. The roar of engine brakes broke the silence every so often. I knew that this might be a bit of a problem as we tried to sleep, but we were feeling content with full bellies and the warm glow of mild sunburn on our shoulders and didn't care . . . at least not yet anyway.

It had been a fantastic afternoon, chilling in paradise. We felt like we were in the Caribbean or on some other tropical island. The thing that made it even better for us was to remind ourselves that we arrived here in our own car. Who would have thought it was possible to reach such a tropical destination simply by pointing your car south?

Day 6

The sky was turning a pale pink when we awoke, and the wind from yesterday had disappeared. The water in the bay was glassy and still. It had been a restless night's sleep with the growl of engine brakes awaking us every few hours. Snuggled in our sleeping bags, we admired the view of the bay while wishing the highway wasn't so close. This campsite rated a nine or ten in campability during waking hours, but only a two or three in sleepability. I guess even in paradise you can't have everything.

Eager to explore the bay before the winds kicked up in the afternoon, we rolled out of bed and loaded up the kayak. There were five or six islands spread out over a mile or two down the bay. Some were only a couple hundred yards from shore, while others were closer to half a mile offshore. The majority of the islands were small, only a few hundred feet around, and devoid of vegetation.

The kayak cut through the smooth water like a knife, and we made good time out to the first island. Paddling around the island, we would pause every so often and peer down through the water at the schools of fish that swam beneath us. At the first island we saw a new kind of fish that we hadn't seen before and called it a parrot fish due to its bright colors.

Kat decided it was time to snorkel and jumped in, leaving me alone in the kayak. With all my weight in the back, the kayak popped a wheelie and I nearly capsized. Taking the hint, I flopped off into the water and pushed the kayak around while snorkeling. There were plenty of fish to watch, so that kept us busy for a while. When we got back in the kayak we realized that with the water being so clear, we could actually see more fish while sitting in the kayak than with our heads in the water.

The next island that we visited looked like it was covered in snow from a distance, but as we got closer the smell told us that the white stuff dripping off the rocks most certainly wasn't snow. Hundreds of sea birds had made the island their home and nesting place. Huge pelicans lined the water's edge, while smaller sea gulls and cormorants peered out of the craggy cliff face.

The birds didn't pay us too much attention until we got a little too close and encroached on the pelicans' personal space. Huge wings beat the air, and soon the entire flock was airborne. Pelicans are not particularly graceful, but their sheer size commands attention—especially when twenty of them take off all at once. We quickly backed off a little and watched from a safer distance as the birds returned to their roosting spots. There must have been over a thousand birds living on the small rock of an island.

By now it was midmorning and we were getting hungry for breakfast, but before heading back we decided to visit one more island. I was glad we did, because this particular island had tons of fish around it— we called it Fish Island due to its huge fish population. We lay back in our seats and watched the fish go about their business for a while before paddling back to camp.

The amazing thing about our morning paddle was the complete solitude that we enjoyed. All morning we had only seen a small fishing boat or two and one other pair of kayakers off in the distance. Pleased with such a beautiful morning paddle, we beached the kayak, walked the twenty feet up the beach to camp, and prepared breakfast.

With a final glance around our nearly perfect campsite, we sighed contentedly and made our way back out to the highway. The next town we would come to was Loreto. Loreto is the oldest settlement in Baja, dating back to 1697 when Jesuit missionaries chose this area for the first mission in California. Today Loreto remains an important link between Ensenada and La Paz. In the late 1970s Fonatur, Mexico's tourism development agency, had big plans for developing the area into a planned mega resort similar to Cabo San Lucas. The development never really took off as was planned, and Loreto has retained its pleasant small-town atmosphere.

We drove into town and did a quick tour without getting out of the truck. I'm sure there are some nice things to see and do in Loreto, but we already had a full afternoon planned and didn't spend much time there. On our way out of town we stopped long enough to fill up with gas at the Pemex station.

The plan for today was to take a side trip into the interior and visit the small town of San Javier. San Javier is a tiny town nestled in the high desert country of central Baja. According to the guidebooks, the town is home to one of the most beautifully preserved mission churches in Baja, and we wanted to check it out.

The dirt road leading out to San Javier weaved around the barren hills and through washed out gullies as it made its way up a steep mountain canyon. The road was rough but thankfully there wasn't much washboard. In several of the gullies there were deep ruts, and I was glad to have high ground clearance.

While crossing a deep arroyo with a small stream flowing down the center, we noticed a sign indicating that there was some rock art nearby. We turned up the arroyo to follow the sign and soon found ourselves in a small dirt parking area next to a tall cliff face. We got out and walked over to the base of the cliff. There was a split-rail fence about five feet away from the base, cordoning off the area. On the rock's surface we could see several faint outlines of stick figures and other designs. The artwork wasn't spectacular or nearly as elaborate as can be found at other sites in Baja, but it was a fun surprise and we enjoyed the stop.

It took us several hours to wind our way up the canyon. On the way we passed some lonely ranches and a tiny one-room church about the size of a one-car garage. Once we were on top of the plateau, the road leveled out and we were able travel much faster—soon we could see San Javier in the distance.

The mission church was the first thing to catch my eye. Against the dark cliffs behind it, the chapel's light grey stone facade shimmered in the sunlight. The town is quite small with a population of only a hundred people or so—tops. The streets are lined with small cottages, and we actually had to wait for a sleeping dog to get out of the road before we could pass.

As we got closer to the church, the dusty road opened up into a broad cobblestone avenue lined with palms and citrus trees. The mission sits at the far end of the plaza—clearly the focal point. In front of the chapel large planters overflowed with flowering purple bushes and bright yellow sunflowers.

Built in 1744, Misión San Javier stands tall and stately with an imposing bell tower jutting into the cloudless blue sky. The walls are constructed of hand hewn stone blocks, and the exterior has ornately carved stone trim around the windows and front door. The remnants of other mission outbuildings and a small cemetery spread out behind the chapel.

We parked the truck near the front entrance and got out to take a look around. There was no one around, so we figured that it was okay to give ourselves a tour. The heavy oak doors were partially open, so we peeked inside. The high ceilings and whitewashed walls made the sanctuary appear much larger than it really was. Rough hand carved pews were set up in neat rows, and a long center aisle let to the altar. Our footsteps echoed off the stone tile floor as we walked down the aisle toward the front of the chapel. Hanging on the wall behind the altar were several age darkened oil paintings of the saints. These paintings were inset into an intricately carved wooden framework gilded with gold leaf. The artwork dated back to the mission days and was very impressive. Not wanting to intrude or overstay our welcome in the sanctuary, we took several photos and then exited.

The mission's grounds were not as well maintained as the chapel, but several buildings were still standing. We wandered around the grounds for a while and took a look at the cemetery. Many of the grave markers were so worn that we couldn't read the lettering.

We took several more pictures of the grounds and then wandered out into the plaza. The place was virtually deserted, with only a few old women conversing in the shade on a nearby patio. A pair of iguanas sat on the wall sunning themselves, and I tried to catch one but they were way too fast for me. The midday sun grew hot, and we looked around for somewhere to buy a soda or something cold to drink. No luck—the only store around looked as if it had been closed for some time, judging by dusty sun bleached Fanta posters in the window and the large padlock on the front door.

The guidebooks were definitely right about San Javier—the mission is an amazing piece of history and well worth the two-hour drive. It was a treat to be able to experience a bit of Baja's history firsthand. San Javier's remote location certainly limits the number of visitors, but those who do make the effort will find the experience very rewarding.

On our way back to the highway, I overtook a little green Ford Fiesta that we had seen leaving town about fifteen minutes before us. The Ford Fiesta is a little compact car with about two inches of clearance and looks a lot like a Geo Metro. I passed him in a cloud of dust and wondered to myself how the Fiesta possibly made it over such rough roads.

I accelerated around him and was soon cruising at 40 mph, flying over the bumps and really moving. I checked my rearview mirror a few minutes later and low and behold, the Fiesta was staying with me. Wanting to stay ahead of him and out of the dust, I bumped it up a level and started driving even more aggressively, but the Fiesta was hanging tough.

I even caught a little bit of air as I shot up and down a steep arroyo bisecting the road, and the truck's suspension compressed all the way—metal to metal. "That will show 'em," I thought to myself, and I watched with anticipation as the Fiesta hit the arroyo.

By this time Kat could tell that I was trying to race the Fiesta and just rolled her eyes. Looking back to see what the Fiesta would do, I saw it hit the arroyo and disappear in a huge cloud of dust. I smugly thought to myself, "Yep, that definitely slowed him down." Feeling pretty good about myself, I watched the Fiesta fall behind . . . for a few minutes anyway, until I checked my rearview mirror and once again saw it gaining ground— amazing!

I began to accelerate again when I noticed that Kat was starting to grip the car door handle even more firmly than normal, and she suggested that maybe we should slow down and let the Fiesta pass us. "No way. There is no possible way that this guy should be able to keep up with us," I commented as we went into a power slide around a dusty hairpin turn with a monster drop-off into the canyon below.

About this time Kat started to get more insistent about not dying, and I conceded to slow down a bit so we didn't fly off the edge of the road. As I reduced my speed to a more sane level, the Fiesta closed the gap and now started to ride my butt as we descended down the canyon. "Man, I hate that guy," I murmured, looking back in the rearview mirror.

Suddenly a wild herd of burros appeared as we rounded a corner, and I had to slam on my brakes. I could tell that the Fiesta really didn't like that, and I smiled to myself. The herd took off down the road, and due to the vertical canyon wall on one side and the cliff on the other, they were forced to run down the road with us following them. Kat was very excited about the burros and started digging around for the camera. I slowed down even further, so as not to frighten them even more than we already had.

The Fiesta was right on my tail now, and I could tell that the driver was getting impatient. At the next pullout I admitted defeat and pulled over. Kat jumped out to take some pictures of the fleeing burros while I hung my head in shame. The Fiesta  zipped around us, and soon all that remained of my struggle to stay out in front was a thin cloud of dust and the smell of hot brakes. I kicked a few rocks in disgust at losing while Kat happily took pictures of the burros and admired the view of the Bahía Concepción in the distance, not caring the least bit that we lost the race to a stinkin' Ford Fiesta.

You just can't compete with Baja drivers—even with their older beat-up vehicles that have no business being on dirt roads. They can still spank any gringo without even trying. The fact of the matter is that the driver of the Fiesta probably didn't even know that we were racing. He was probably just going along doing his normal thing without giving a second thought to the gringo that got in his way.

On several occasions during the trip we came across a beautiful beach with wonderful camping, but due to our lack of four-wheel drive we had to seek a spot with firmer ground. As we looked longingly at the prime spot and cursed our two-wheel drive truck, we would see a Mexican family camped at the water's edge with their beat-up '82 Honda Civic. How they made it across the deep soft beach sand is a mystery, but I knew that if I tried the same thing we would be stuck in a heartbeat.

Another time, while exploring a burly dirt road with huge ruts and steep embankments, we noticed a small compact car of some sort camped along the side of the road. It appeared to be in good condition, and I marveled at how a car with less than three inches of ground clearance could possibly have negotiated the drive out there. I imagine that these desert driving skills must be learned as a young child and passed on from one generation to another.

Back on the highway we turned south and began to look for a nice camping spot on the map. Highway 1 follows the coast very closely, and there are some great views of the Loreto Bay National Marine Park. The Marine Park is a protected wildlife area that consists of about thirty-five miles of coastline and extends several miles offshore to include the islands of Isla Danazante and Isla Carmen.

We found a nice camping spot at Playa Juancalito. This beach is situated in a large cove with several small fish camps on one side and an empty stretch of beach on the other. The part of beach where we camped juts out into the bay and is quite secluded. Compared with our magnificent campsite the night before, Playa Juancalito was not quite as pretty but was much farther from the highway and more isolated. We found a nice little spot near the water and pulled in and set up camp. The bay was tranquil and quiet, and we relaxed in our camp chairs admiring the view.

The only downside of this camp was the amount of trash and litter around. This was something that we had noticed in many of the campsites that we had used while in Baja. It was sad to see so much trash in such beautiful remote areas. There seems to be very little stigma associated with littering, and subsequently much of Baja has trash strewn about on the ground. This phenomenon is seen in many third world countries, and until the culture of littering is broken, candy wrappers, broken bottles, and empty chip bags will continue to ruin otherwise pristine wilderness areas.

Dinner consisted of frying up the remaining fish and squeezing fresh limes over the fillets. While eating we watched several small fishing boats return with their day's catch and beach themselves near the fish camps. The men hauled large coolers up the beach and yelled greetings to each another. They gathered around in small groups — talking, comparing each other's catch, and joking around.

After dinner I felt the call of nature, so I got the trusty roll of TP and little red shovel and wandered into the palm grove hoping to find an outhouse or a comfy place to take care of business. So far during the trip, in the various places we had camped, we had found some of the most disgusting outhouses on the planet. Many times the convenience of the outhouse was far outweighed by the sanitary concerns, and we opted for the open-air experience.

Tonight I was feeling lucky, and low and behold, there in a clearing stood the outhouse. From a distance it looked spacious and fairly well built, which I can assure you is not the norm. As I walked closer I could tell that this outhouse was going to be special. It had a concrete foundation and a thatched palm roof. Opening the door, I braced myself for whatever might be inside.

To my surprise the concrete floor was actually pretty clean, and the smell was well within tolerable limits. The unexpected cleanliness wasn't the only surprise — this outhouse was what many would refer to as a "two-holer." The beauty of this particular outhouse's design was that instead of the two seats being side by side with a divider between them, as one might imagine, the two toilet seats were directly across from each other. Not only were the two seats opposite each other, but they were so closely placed together that if two people were to use the outhouse at the same time, their knees would nearly be touching as they gazed into each other's eyes.

I laughed the whole time I was using the outhouse and imagined how hilarious and uncomfortable it would be if there was someone sitting directly in front of me using the other hole. I actually ran back to camp and dragged Kat over to the outhouse to see the marvelous design. We both had a good laugh and theorized that this particular outhouse design must have looked much better on paper than it turned out to be once it was built.

Still chuckling at the outhouse, we wandered back to camp through the waning light. We pulled out the chairs and sat down to write in the journal and read our books. We were now over two thirds of the way down the peninsula, and I found myself wishing that we had more time to explore and enjoy Baja. Time was flying along—I couldn't believe that we had been gone almost a week.

As the stars began to appear on the horizon one by one, we retired from our chairs and lay in bed reading our books and watching the moon rise over the water. The palms swayed gently in the breeze and all was quiet. It was a perfect ending to a wonderful day.

Map of Days 7, 8 and 9

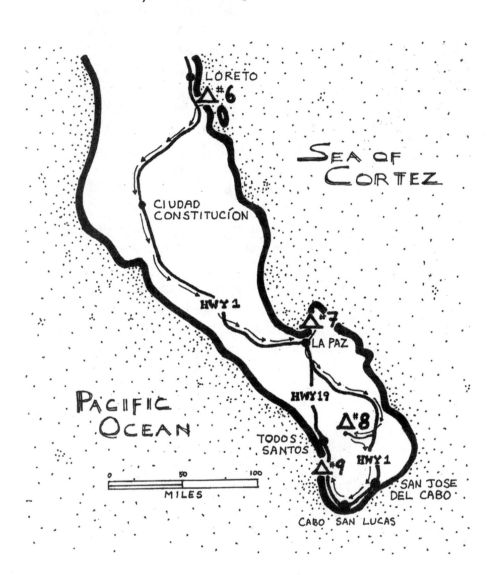

Day 7

The smooth water in the bay reflected the soft yellows and pinks of the predawn sky like a mirror. The outline of Isla Danazante was black and dark as the glow of the rising sun spread up behind its jagged peaks. The cloud-streaked sky had tinges of purple at the edges, and a thin mist hung on the water like a protective blanket. It was still early and my sleeping bag was warm and comfortable, but I got up long enough to snap a quick picture to capture the sunrise. My stirrings woke Kat, and we sat up in the back of the truck with our sleeping bags wrapped around us, experiencing the awakening of a new day.

The purr of an outboard engine firing up rolled across the bay as the fishermen readied their boats. Their fishing boats are small aluminum skiffs, only ten or fifteen feet long with open bows. Styrofoam coolers, nets, and buoys rest in the bottom. Each boat is crewed by two fishermen — the driver who runs the outboard and the net thrower who stands in the bow. The boats are fast and speed along, barely skimming the surface as they race from one fishing spot to another.

When they reach a spot that might contain fish, they slow way down and the net guy stands up in the bow of the boat, net in hand, and peers into the water. He calls out directions to the motor guy as he tries to position the boat over a school of fish. At the perfect moment the net guy tosses the net off the front of the boat into the water and then pulls it back in, hopefully with a few fish in it. This process is then repeated over and over until the school scatters, and then the fishermen speed off looking for a new fishing spot.

One of the boats sped over closer to us, slowed, and we were able to watch the fishermen at their craft. They moved quietly and efficiently, tossing the net, pulling it in, and tossing it out again—all in a steady rhythm.

Also out on the water this morning was another type of fisherman, the pelican. Pelicans employ a method that is similar to their human counterparts as they endeavor to get their next meal. They fly slowly over the water in a large group, and when they spot a school of fish they fall awkwardly out of the sky one by one into a steep dive, crashing into the water with beaks wide open. Moments later all the pelicans are bobbing in the water, craning their necks as they swallow the fish from their large pouched bills. It was fascinating to watch both the fishermen and the pelicans try to earn their daily bread alongside one another. Still in our sleeping bags, we sat for about twenty minutes and observed the dance between the fishermen and the sea.

After some breakfast we got the kayak ready and loaded up to go out for the morning. Sliding into the bay, we paddled out around the southern point and headed down the coast toward Puerto Escondido.

Puerto Escondido is a small protected harbor with a very narrow entrance that could easily be missed if you weren't looking closely. Once inside the narrow entrance, the anchorage opens up and can accommodate quite a few boats. I can never resist checking out sailboats, so we pulled in to have a look. We stopped on the breakwater and made our way over the slippery rocks to peer into the harbor. The harbor was about half full of boats, and the masts swayed slightly in the breeze. The clinking of the rigging slapping against the masts floated across the water as the boats rocked gently from side to side in the swell.

A loud snort and whooshing sound behind us quickly turned our attention away from the sailboats. Spinning around to see what was making the noise, I nearly lost my footing on the slippery rocks and almost fell over. Recovering my balance, I scanned the water for a second or two before spotting them—dolphins! They were about twenty yards off shore and moving along at a leisurely pace, for dolphins that is. We rushed back to the kayak and hopped in, ready to give chase. As Kat fumbled for the camera, I paddled madly in an attempt to catch up to the dolphins.

Even though the dolphins were probably moving along at a comfortable speed for them, it was full speed ahead for me. I was barely able to keep up with them. It

was a family of four dolphins—two adults and two juveniles. It was really exciting to see dolphins in the wild and to be able to get so close to them. Their sleek black bodies slid through the water effortlessly as they arched their backs and kicked slowly.

By now the sweat was dripping off the tip of my nose, and I was getting tired. It was hard for Kat to time the shutter delay of the digital camera with their surfacings, and I wasn't sure how much longer I could keep up with the dolphins. A few cross words might have been exchanged in the heat of the battle. Something about someone's ability to work the camera, to which another comment was made about another person's ability to steer the kayak in a straight line.

In spite of some hurt feelings, we persevered and got some great pictures before the pod left us behind. Once the excitement of the chase wore off, we apologized to each other and sat back in our seats, reveling in our amazing dolphin experience.

Now that the chase was completed, we looked around and realized that we had paddled ourselves pretty far out into the bay. A few miles offshore, Isla Danazante stood tall and imposing. We were about a third of the way there already, so we decided to continue on out to the island. It took us about an hour to reach the island, and it was definitely the farthest we had paddled away from shore. For us as inexperienced sea kayakers, it seemed like a daunting task to get out to the island, but for the more experienced kayaker it wouldn't be a problem.

We found a beach to land on near the northern tip and went ashore. The island's tall rocky peaks towered over our beach, and much of the shoreline was inaccessible due to the sheer cliffs that dropped straight into the water. Donning our snorkels and fins, we left the kayak on the beach and swam out into the water. The water was full of fish and other sea creatures. Away from the sediment and pollution of the mainland, the clarity of the water was terrific.

We saw several new types of tropical fish and a new type of starfish. These starfish were a deep red and covered in small spiny orange bumps. We took turns diving to the bottom and checking them out up close. The shallow sea floor near shore was littered with them.

A few minutes later Kat grew alarmed as she found herself surrounded by a bunch of small jellyfish. They had pale pink translucent bodies about half an inch long, and their tentacles hung in the water like wispy threads of cotton candy. Thankfully the jellies didn't seem to sting much, and Kat was able to swim right through them.

We returned to the kayak after snorkeling around for an hour or so. Lying on the beach, looking back across the bay to the mainland, we began to wonder if it had been such a good idea to have paddled out so far. From our vantage point out on the island, the mainland now looked pretty far away, and I knew that it would be a long paddle back.

It was a workout to get back to shore. We tried games such as power 100s, 200s, and finally 300s. This game consists of lowering your head, digging in, and giving the proper number of power strokes without looking up. The purpose of doing this is so that once you finally look up, you will be amazed at how much closer you are to your destination. This is a throwback to our days as rafting guides where we would ask our clients to do a certain number of paddle strokes before they could rest for a while. The difference was that while rafting we usually only asked for power 10s or 20s.

Playing the power stroke game helped, but it seemed like even after doing a power 300 we were still really far away from shore. Not wanting to tire ourselves out too much, we took our time and tried to keep a steady pace. About an hour and a half later we limped back to camp, tired but glad that we had made the trek out to Isla Danazante.

The scenery between Loreto and La Paz is for the most part unremarkable. The rolling hills and mountains flatten out, and the larger cactuses and desert plants give way to smaller shrubs. The highway veers back to the center of the peninsula, and the road is straight and flat.

About an hour or so south of Loreto, Highway 1 runs right through the center of Ciudad Constitución. Ciudad Constitución is a fairly sizeable city with an agricultural economy. It is southern Baja's largest agricultural area, and its fields are irrigated with well water that is sucked from deep below the desert sand. The patchwork of cultivated fields flew by as we sped toward La Paz. Soon the brilliant greens of the young alfalfa were replaced once again by the browns of the desert. Without much to look at we made good time, averaging about 110 km per hour.

I took a nap after Ciudad Constitución, and Kat drove the rest of the way to La Paz. It only took us about four hours to get from Loreto to La Paz. It was nice to take a break from driving. Up to this point I had done the majority of the driving while Kat took care of the mapping and direction giving. From previous road trips we had determined that this was the best arrangement. Even still, sometimes I got tired of driving and we tried switching roles.

On several occasions during the trip I tried to be the navigator and work the map, but it only ended in disaster. I would somehow manage to miss a critical turn or important item of information and get Kat hopelessly lost. After multiple navigational mistakes and the following tense moments, we decided to stick with what we are good at—me in the driver's seat taking directions, and Kat in the passenger's seat giving them.

As we neared La Paz Kat pulled over and I slid back into the driver's seat. Bracing myself for the onslaught of a big city, I adjusted the mirrors and got in my defensive driving position—hands tightly gripping the wheel and eyes darting to the mirrors, watching for any rogue cars. Kat smiled and pulled out the map. It was time to start looking at what La Paz had to offer.

The city of La Paz has a lot of Baja history. It was the spot where Spaniards first set foot on the peninsula in 1533. The Indians immediately killed them, and for nearly two hundred years the Spanish tried unsuccessfully to establish a colony in La Paz. It wasn't until 1829 when Loreto was destroyed by storm that the city actually took hold.

Today La Paz is a thriving city with a population of 185,000 and is the biggest city in Baja Sur. It has a long walkway along the waterfront, and the city stretches back into the hills, overlooking the hook shaped bay. In spite of its large size, La Paz is a friendly city and didn't seem too large or intimidating when we first pulled in.

We parked the truck on a side street near the water and got out to walk along the waterfront and stretch our legs. A white sand beach runs alongside the wide pedestrian path as it hugs the contours of the bay. Palm trees swayed and rustled their fronds in the warm breeze and cast tall thin shadows across the hot pavement. A large statue of Cristoból Columbus guarded the walkway in front of the marina where several large yachts floated peacefully. La Paz is definitely a touristy place with lots of shops and brightly painted hotels that line the waterfront.

La Paz's international airport, beautiful beaches, and duty-free port, coupled with its temperate climate, make it a popular vacation destination. Another factor that makes La Paz such a vibrant vacation spot is the ferry that connects it to mainland Mexico. The ferry crosses the Sea of Cortez and is mainly used by Mexicans who come to vacation in Baja. La Paz sees more Mexican vacationers than American tourists for this reason. But with that said, there were still bunches of American tourists around.

We laughed at how easy it was to for us to pick out the tourists walking down the streets — they were so obvious. There were middle-aged white guys with their polo shirts tucked into khaki shorts. Their wives clung to their sides, trying to look ten years younger with their hair dyed a "natural blonde" and their skin an even bronze color from the pre-trip visits to the tanning booth. My favorite part of the tourist look was the white socks and penny loafers that most of the men seemed to favor.

This was the first time we had really seen tourists since crossing the border up in Tijuana and Ensenada, and in some strange way I felt like we were superior to common "Tourista." These people had hopped on a plane that morning and arrived all shiny and clean, while for the past week we had been driving, camping, and experiencing a Baja that they would never know existed. It may sound silly, but I felt like we had earned our way and by doing so were more deserving of Baja's beauty.

We ate dinner at La Fonda, which was a cute hole-in-the-wall restaurant that came highly recommended by one of the guidebooks. The ambience was quaint and relaxing, with the dinning area under a small covered patio area. Sweet smelling Bougainvillea vines hung down from overhead. Our waiter was friendly and the food was excellent. We only spent about twenty-two dollars on sodas, appetizers, and the main course.

After our meal the owner came over to our table and we chatted for a while. He said that things were slow this time of year and that the majority of his business came during the winter in the form of tour buses stopping by. He was very gracious and wished us well on the rest of our travels in Baja. Then he disappeared back into the kitchen.

Finishing up with dinner, we pulled out the map and discussed where to spend the night. We took a leisurely stroll back to the truck and then drove along the bay until we reached the edge of town. We passed the ferry dock and the large Pemex oil refinery as we made our way out toward the northeastern part of the bay to get to our camping spot. We found a spot that was relatively secluded in the dunes overlooking the beach and set up camp.

There were several other groups camping in and among the dunes, but we still had plenty of privacy. It was nice not to have to cook dinner and to be able to pull into camp, set up our camp chairs, and just relax.

As the sun set over the water, we were graced with one of the most fantastic sunsets I have ever seen. The sky was an explosion of pinks and purples highlighted with oranges and yellows bursting from the horizon. We sat in amazement as the brilliant colors filled the sky and then slowly evolved and transformed into deeper richer tones of red and purple as the sun sunk farther and farther into the horizon. We were able to take several pictures of the sunset to preserve it on film. The pictures turned out magnificently, but they paled in comparison to the real event.

In the growing darkness I flipped on my headlamp and spent about an hour writing in the journal. By this point in the trip I was really starting to get the hang of writing in the journal. It gave me the opportunity to reflect on and remember all the fun and interesting things we had done that day. I have never really been one to keep a journal, and it surprised me how much I enjoyed doing it. The words flowed effortlessly onto the pages, and I found myself looking forward to recording my thoughts each night. Writing in the journal became an important part of my day and shaped my Baja experience, because without it so much of the journey would have been forgotten or lost due to the enormity of the trip.

While I wrote Kat tidied up the truck and consolidated our food Tupperwares. Kat made the trip so much easier with her strong organizational skills and patience in packing things up each morning. She is a seasoned adventurer and can handle even the most primitive camping conditions without complaint. Over the years she has proven herself to be a super camper and traveling companion.

With my alternative work schedule, we have noticed that it is difficult to find friends who have the same amount of time or similar commitment to recreation. Subsequently, most of the time we hang out together and find activities that we both like to do. We look at other couples who don't share similar interests or hang out together and wonder if they know what they are missing.

After I finished with the journal for the evening, Kat and I sat back in our chairs overlooking the beach and commented on how quickly the days had passed and how much we had enjoyed the trip so far. I was already more than a little melancholy that we were so close to the tip of the peninsula, because that meant that we would soon have to turn around and head home.

The stresses of work and real life felt like a forgotten distant memory, but at the same time it didn't seem like we had been gone long enough. It made me sad to think that we would soon have to return home, but these thoughts were quickly forgotten as we pulled out the map and books to plan the next day's activities.

Day 8

There was a slight breeze blowing across the beach when we awoke, and the sun was already up over the water shining brightly in our eyes. The wind had kicked up in the night, blowing sand onto our sleeping bags, but nothing like the hurricane winds of Bahía de Los Angeles, and we had slept through it for the most part. During the night we were awakened by what we thought was the bark of a sea lion, but we couldn't see him out in the waves, so it could have been something else making the noise.

We lounged about in our sleeping bags for a while, enjoying the warm sun on our faces. Kat finally got up first, as she always does, and started on breakfast. I eventually joined her for breakfast, and after we had eaten we decided to pack up the truck.

As I walked around the truck I noticed that a rear tire was completely flat. "Hmmm . . ." I thought, "that's not too good." I got down and gave it a quick inspection but couldn't see any punctures or holes. Luckily I had given some thought to the subject of flat tires before we had embarked on this adventure, and I had had the forethought to bring some Fix-A-Flat cans to inflate tires. I dug around in several Tuppewares until I found one of them and then tried to inflate the tire. After a couple of false starts I got it to work, and the tire looked good as new.

Driving back towards La Paz for a mile or two we reached our morning's destination — Playa Balandra. This was a beach that several of the guidebooks recommended for snorkeling. To get there we had to take a small spur road for about half a mile to a secluded parking area.

Our truck was the only vehicle in the parking lot and there was no one around. Pulling the kayak off the rack, I surveyed the beach and cove—it looked fantastic. Aquamarine water lapped gently against a white powder beach, and several pelicans squawked shrilly in the distance.

The sand was hot under our bare feet as we dragged the kayak across the beach to the lagoon. The water was very shallow— only about twelve inches deep—for about two hundred feet off the beach. The drop-off where the sea floor fell away was clearly marked as the pale clear water deepened into a rich tropical blue.

The warm water sloshed around our ankles as we pushed the kayak into the shallow water. We tried to get into the kayak too soon and found ourselves resting on the bottom. Instead of getting out and walking like normal people would, we spent twice as much effort pushing with our paddles and scooting across the shallows. Although not very efficient, it was fun and we eventually made it out into deeper water.

The sunlight danced across the top of the water, creating a mosaic of shimmering hues of blue. Once we reached deeper water we paddled out into the bay toward a coral head in the center of the lagoon. It was the most coral we had seen so far, and we hoped there would be lots of fish around it.

We were not disappointed. From our vantage point sitting atop the kayak, we could see fish darting underneath us as we neared the coral. We put on our snorkels and masks and over the side we went. We took turns being in charge of dragging the kayak above us as we explored the reef beneath us. Once again, we saw several varieties of fish that were previously unknown to us, and found ourselves wishing again that we had a fish identification card. We took turns with the underwater camera and dove down  deep to get close-ups of the new fish. It was fantastic snorkeling, and the bay was beautiful. Best of all, we had it all to ourselves.

After passing a good portion of the morning exploring the reef, we paddled over to a secluded beach on the far side of the cove to take a rest. The sun was bright and we lay out for a while catching some rays and hanging out on the beach. It was something out of the movies to have such a beautiful spot all to ourselves for the whole morning.

On the way back into La Paz the road followed the coast, and at times the water was only a few feet away. As we were driving Kat exclaimed, "Hey, there's a dolphin right over there in the water." I turned my head to get a better view and low and behold, she was right. A dolphin *was* swimming alongside of us not thirty feet out in the water. How cool is that to see a dolphin in the wild, while still in your vehicle, and a moving vehicle at that?!

Back in town we found an Internet place and spent a few minutes emailing our families to update them on our progress. The girl at the counter was friendly and let us plug in our digital camera battery charger while we used the Internet. The Internet continued to be one of the best bargains in Baja — only ten pesos for the hour. The battery wasn't fully charged by the time we were done, so we took a walk around the neighborhood while it finished charging.

We had tried to find a tire pressure gauge for sale in several different cities during the trip, and so far we hadn't had any luck, but with the current tire problem we figured we had better try again. We visited an auto parts store, a gas station, and a hardware store, but once again the tire pressure gauge proved elusive.

Giving up on the tire pressure gauge, we changed our tactics and began looking for some lunch. We found an excellent taco stand a few blocks away. We ate fish tacos in the shade of a large tree and did some people watching. In addition to the fish tacos, we also tried a shrimp and a lobster taco. The lobster taco was especially tasty.

By now our battery was done charging, so we walked back to the Internet place and collected it. We filled up the truck at the Pemex station and, after getting a little lost in downtown La Paz, made our way back out to Highway 1. The streets weren't too crowded, but the other drivers' disregard for all traffic laws made me nervous, and I had to assume my defensive driving position.

The plan for the day was to travel down the highway for an hour or so till we reached the town of Santiago, where we would take a side road to our destination of Agua Caliente. Agua Caliente is a small ranching village at the base of the Sierra de La Laguna Mountains. Agua Caliente translates as hot water and derives its name from a hot spring that is located outside of town.

The dirt road that turned off the highway leading toward Agua Caliente was a dream—smooth, with no washboard at all. We reviewed the directions given in the guidebooks and hoped it would be pretty obvious where we should go, because the directions were pretty vague. Once we reached the village, which consisted of a small one-room school, an even smaller church, and several houses gathered around a central plaza, it became clear that it wouldn't be an easy task to find the hot spring. There were several dirt roads all leading off in different directions, and all of them were unmarked.

After trying several of the wrong roads, we got a little discouraged and figured we would try one or two more, but after that we would have to go with Plan B. Plan B was asking someone for directions. I tried to remember the word for hot spring in Spanish and eventually had to look it up, but I still wasn't satisfied with the clarity of the translation. In addition to not being confident in my ability to communicate what I was looking for, the few locals we saw peering out of their windows at us didn't look super friendly. So I wasn't excited about the prospect of having to knock on some random door and ask for directions.

We decided that we would give it one more try before resorting to Plan B. The last road we tried led us to a ranch with several horse corrals and a gate blocking the road. Discouraged at taking yet another wrong turn, I looked for somewhere to turn around. Not wanting to intrude on the ranch, I tried to do a ninety-point turn in the narrow road.

While I attempted this, Kat noticed that a smaller road continued on around the ranch. We keep going a little farther, and the road soon dead-ended in the mouth of a narrow canyon that was blocked by a concrete flood control dam. We paused and I saw a rancher walking across the dam heading our way, so I figured that maybe he could direct us to the hot spring. We started talking and he indicated that the hot spring was actually just on the other side of the dam.

The rancher explained that the hot water gushes from a crack in the canyon wall and then mixes with the cooler water of the stream that flows into it, creating a nice swimming hole. I asked him if it was okay if we camped here, and he said that it would be fine. He continued on his way, and we got out to explore. I climbed up on the dam and could see a large pool of emerald green water with a small stream flowing into it from up the canyon.

I was totally stoked that we managed to find this place after taking so many wrong turns—what a stroke of luck. We changed into our swimsuits and climbed up and over the dam. The pool was ringed with thick green moss and smelled strongly of sulfur. We were both a little hesitant to enter the water, but I went first, breaking through the layer of moss. The water was lukewarm around the edges of the pool, but as I got in and started to walk toward the far side where the spring was, I began to hit some hotter pockets of water.

Hundreds of small fish maybe an inch long swarmed around my legs and tickled me. I wasn't sure how much I liked all those fish attacking my legs, but I pressed on anyway. As I drew closer to the spring, the water started to get much warmer and felt like hot bath water. Someone had built a circular rock wall around the crack that the hot water flowed out of to form a primitive hot tub. I sank in up to my neck and sat back to enjoy the hot water.

Kat was still standing at the water's edge waiting to see what happened to me—providing moral support, of course. "Come on in, the water's fine," I called, and she slowly waded out into the water. Kat wasn't too sure about all the small fish swarming around her legs either but kept advancing anyway. Soon we were both chilling in the "hot tub" and admiring the rugged canyon in the fading afternoon sunlight.

Once the wrinkles started to form on our fingers, we decided it was time to get out and explore farther up the canyon. The stream meandered through large granite boulders, and lush green vegetation ringed the deeper pools of murky water. The peaks of the Sierra de La Laguna Mountains soared over the canyon walls, hazy in the afternoon heat, creating a washed-out purple backdrop. The canyon was alive with the cooing of doves and other desert birds calling to each other.

Scrambling up the mostly dry riverbed, we imagined what this place would be like during the annual flooding. It would definitely be a sight to behold. We stopped in the shade of a small grove of palms and admired the uniqueness of the landscape around us.

Baja's interior is a land of extremes. I looked down at the cool water trickling through the rocks and the lush moss that floated on the surface of the pools, and then I glanced up to the canyon walls where scrubby desert plants and cactuses somehow manage to thrive in bone dry desert sand. The contrast was so stark, and yet it all fit together perfectly.

Walking back down the canyon, I decided to go for another dip in the hot spring while Kat returned to the truck to start on dinner. While soaking in the pool, I kept myself amused by trying to catch the small fish in my cupped hands and scoop them up out of the water. I occasionally caught one, but they were fast little guys and usually jumped out of my hands before I got them out of the water. I eventually got out and made my way up the dam and back to camp.

For dinner we cooked up some Thai Peanut Noodles. Dinner turned out pretty good, and it was nice to sit in the shade of the canyon walls and feel the warmth radiating off the sun scorched rocks. One advantage of camping away from the coast was the absence of the flies and bugs that are much more plentiful at the beach. I didn't miss the flies one bit.

This was our first time camping away from the beach, and it felt kind of strange to be away from the ocean. Instead of the crash of surf on the beach during dinner, we could hear the mooing of cattle as they crashed through the underbrush across the river. I hoped that none of them would wander into our camp during the night and trample us while we slept.

After dinner was cleaned up, we slipped into our usual post dinner routine of journal writing and reading our books by headlamp. The sky was clear and we fell asleep under a full canopy of glistening stars.

Day 9

It was still dark and the stars were shining brightly when I was abruptly awakened by the crunch of tires as they came to a stop near our truck. I was instantly wide awake and concerned with the prospect of having visitors during the middle of the night in such a secluded and remote location.

Several scenarios played themselves out in my mind—none of them good. I quickly looked around for something to use as a weapon, if it came to that, and all I could come up with was a paperback book. Doh! I kicked myself as I desperately wished I had thought about this sort of situation beforehand and had a more suitable weapon at hand.

Paperback book held at the ready, I apprehensively peered over the bed of the truck as a guy in a cowboy hat hopped out of a beat-up ranching truck and strode toward us. "Oh, crap," I thought, "this is definitely not good." The cowboy took four long strides in our direction until he veered around us and headed over to the dam. Clicking on his LED headlamp, he climbed up the dam, made his way over to the irrigation gate, and began to turn the wheel.

About this time I remembered to breathe again, and I sucked in a gasping breath. The oxygen burst helped my still groggy mind connect the dots and figure out that he was just turning on the irrigation water and not interested in a couple of gringos camped out in the canyon.

I flopped back down into my sleeping bag still a little short of breath but feeling very relieved. Kat stirred and sleepily asked if everything was all right. "Sure, sure, I got it under control," I squeaked, then clearing my throat and saying much more authoritatively, "Just a rancher turning on the irrigation valve. You can go back to sleep." By now my pulse had returned to a much more healthy speed and I mused, "How is it that a rural rancher, out here in the boonies of Baja, has discovered the technology of LED headlamps?"

As I drifted back into slumber land, I wondered if maybe he had found it at this very camp spot, forgotten in a panic by some poor gringo camper as he was hastily fleeing camp in the middle of the night, trying to get away from the strange ranching truck that had just pulled up.

It was already warm when we woke up, and the far side of the canyon was aglow in the early morning light. We ate a quick breakfast, packed up our things, and got ready to leave. We had a big day planned and needed to get an early start.

We would reach the tip of the peninsula before nightfall and had lots to see and do. On the way back toward the town of Agua Caliente, we passed a herd of cattle on the road and waved to the rancher as we went by.

Soon we were back on Highway 1, heading south toward Cabo San José. Kat likes stopping at the little towns to see what they are like, so we took a quick detour to visit the town of Miraflores. It's hard to blend in and pretend you aren't a tourist when you have a bright yellow kayak strapped to the roof, and we got quite a few stares in the smaller villages we visited. They could spot us a mile away.

We noticed that there were lots of kids walking around in their Sunday best and carrying party bags. We guessed that it was some sort of holiday or maybe time for the annual village fiesta, but we weren't sure. Kat commented that the Mexican kids are so cute and had a fun time waving to them. Most of them shyly smiled and looked at their feet, but a few of the bolder ones waved back. It was still too early for most of the shops to open, so we drove through town and then went back out to the highway without stopping.

A few miles north of Cabo San José, the highway widened and turned into a four-lane freeway. We braced ourselves for the onslaught of civilization that we were about to enter. Cabo San José is the beginning of a large metropolitan area that stretches across the bottom of the peninsula to Cabo San Lucas. We were now entering the land of the tourist.

The urban sprawl grew up around us as we entered the city of Cabo San José. Our first stop was at the botanical garden of Cacti-Mundo, translated as Cactus World. We parked on the street, got out, paid our sixty-peso admission, and walked inside. The garden was a beautiful arrangement of carefully manicured walks and hundreds of varieties of cactuses.

Although the garden wasn't large, the sheer number of cactuses was overwhelming. The tropical sun beat down on us, and even though it was still mid morning, we were already sweating. We wandered around the garden, picking out our favorite cactuses and chasing the lizards down the paths. A golf course surrounded by brightly painted condominiums was located behind the garden and reminded us that the American dollar rules supreme, even in Baja.

Back on the freeway hotels and large resorts began to spring up as we neared Cabo San Lucas. We passed the airport and actually got stuck in some traffic for a few minutes. That was certainly a change from the lonely back roads that we had become accustomed to.

About halfway to Cabo San Lucas we stopped at a beach named Playa Santa María. The guidebook recommended it as a lesser known beach with great snorkeling. To reach it we had to exit the freeway and cross back underneath it on a dirt road that led us to a parking lot. The parking lot was full of cars, and a uniformed security guard directed us where to park. We looked at each other and wondered what the more popular beaches would be like.

The beach was a short walk away, so we loaded up our backpack, beach towels, and some lunch and started off across the sand. The path led us to a horseshoe shaped cove with a coarse white sand beach. It was fairly crowded with both American and Mexican tourists, but we found an empty spot to lay out our stuff. After the seclusion we had experienced so far in Baja, any beach that we had to share with anyone seemed crowded, although in hindsight this beach really wasn't so bad. It was much less crowded than any southern California beach.

Small clear waves broke on the sand, and the water deepened to a brilliant turquoise blue farther out. A large catamaran bobbed in the cove as a herd of tourists snorkeled around the boat. Soon after we arrived, someone on the sailboat blew a whistle; all the snorkelers returned to the catamaran and soon it sailed out of the cove. While we were there on the beach several other boats full of tourists entered, snorkeled for a while, and then left.

The sun was intense and even with sunscreen I could feel myself burning. I felt like there was a huge heat lamp pointed directly at me. We were definitely in the tropics now. Feeling the need to escape from the relentless sun, we decided to get in the water and swim around.

The snorkeling was excellent, and in spite of the many people in the water there were fish everywhere. I learned, after the fact, that many of the tourist boats give their clients food to feed the fish, which explained the millions of fish around. We saw a couple of new fish, and I tried to take pictures of them with the underwater camera. Even with all the people in the water, the clarity was fantastic and it was some of the best snorkeling we had done so far.

Back on shore we lay on our beach towels enjoying the water, sun, and people around us. We were soon accosted by one of the Mexicans who walk up and down the beaches trying to sell his wares. These walking salesmen are numerous and have perfected their selling technique. They have selling down to a science, and most gringos don't stand a chance. These guys are always super friendly, and before you know it they have all their wares placed before you and are doing their best to separate you from your money.

One guy sat down next to us and tried to sell us silver bracelets for at least fifteen minutes, but we held strong and somehow escaped buying anything. Not minutes after that guy left, a new salesman stopped by and starting chatting with us. He introduced himself as Pedro. The next thing we knew he was showing us all of the carved wooden figures he was selling.

Pedro already had an advantage over the previous guy, because he was selling something that I might want to buy. Although I am usually not excited by knickknacks, these carvings were very beautiful, and I was instantly impressed. The carvings were made of ironwood, which has a deep rich brown color, and they were polished to a high gloss. He had all sorts of carvings: whales, turtles, pelicans, fish, many other animals, and cactuses. They ranged in size from only a couple of inches to over a foot tall.

The collection presented before us in the sand was impressive, but the catch was that the carvings were quite expensive. Pedro went on at great lengths about how he had spent hours hand carving them himself and that each one was special. Thinking that I could possibly get a good deal and that they would be fun reminders of our trip, we selected two cactuses, one big and the other small, and a medium sized carving of a pelican.

Pedro did some quick math in his head and told us that the three carvings would normally cost us nine hundred pesos but that he would give me the "good price" of eight hundred. I looked in my wallet to see what I actually had and counted three hundred pesos and a ten-dollar bill. Now keep in mind that eight hundred pesos is almost eighty dollars, and to some tourists that would be chump change, but for us it was a lot. So I told Pedro, "Look, all I have is three hundred pesos and ten dollars — its all yours for the three pieces."

He hemmed and hawed for a few minutes about how it was too little and then told us that we could have two of the carvings for that price but not three. I stood firm, saying "It's the three pieces or no deal," and negotiations stagnated. Not wanting to lose the sale, he packed up the other carvings slowly while trying to convince me of the good deal that he was giving me.

When he saw that I wouldn't budge, he looked around and asked, "Do you have anything else of value that you can throw in to sweeten the deal?" He then went on to suggest, "A radio or something else of value?" But I told him I didn't have anything to trade.

Again, I offered him the three hundred pesos and the ten-dollar bill, and he shook his head. Then one of his seller buddies came over to see if he could help. It's the classic switch-a-roo trick that so many car dealerships use to lure you into buying more than you can afford. The new guy listened sympathetically to what was going on and then reopened the avenue of seeing if we had something else of value to throw into the deal.

They asked, "What about your CamelBak?"
"No!"
"Binoculars?"
"No."
"Snorkel gear?"
"No."

And finally they asked "your camera?"

"No way!"

Once again, we were at an impasse. By now, I was kind of getting tired of the whole thing and didn't care too much if the sale fell through. Pedro, in one final attempt to make the sale, looked around in desperation, eyed the beach towel we were sitting on, and said, "Throw in the beach towel, and the cactuses and pelican are yours." Kat and I exchanged glances and the deal was done. We got up, brushed the sand off our bright green Wal-Mart special, and handed it over. Pedro carefully folded it up, put it in his bag, and wandered off — sale complete.

We congratulated ourselves on a job well done and admired our new souvenirs. Later in Cabo San Lucas we found a whole bunch of the same carvings in numerous gift shops around town. Pedro must have been very busy hand carving them all. Even if our carvings weren't originals or quite as special as we had thought, we still thought they were super cool. The experience of buying the carvings on the beach alone made it worth buying from Pedro. As a bonus, the carvings were even more expensive in town, so we took comfort in the fact that we got them at a good price.

The sun was beating down on us, and without a towel to sit on anymore we decided to pack it up and head back to the truck. On our way out of the parking lot we gave a tip to the security guard, as is the custom, and got back on the freeway.

It took us about thirty minutes to reach the actual city of Cabo San Lucas. On the way we passed a bunch of fancy beachfront hotels and resorts. There were definitely more American tourists than we had seen previously.

They were easy to spot as they drove by in their shiny compact rental cars. The first thing we noticed was the crumpled road map taking up the majority of the passenger's side of the windshield. Then as we looked closer we could see the look of panic on the driver's pale face as a beat-up Pinto sped around him on the right. Then the flash of Hawaiian shirts from the couple in the back seat caught my eye, and our suspicions were confirmed — gringo tourists.

Cabo San Lucas is a huge city, teeming with life. Several gigantic cruise ships sat out in the harbor, dwarfing all the other boats. The streets were filled with tourists wandering from shop to shop, and the traffic was heavy. We drove along the waterfront toward the arch, El Arco, for which Cabo is well known. El Arco is located on a rocky outcropping that forms a narrow peninsula at the tip of the harbor. At the very end of this point is a little rock called Land's End, which is considered to be the southernmost tip of Baja.

We were hoping to kayak around the peninsula, but we soon realized that there was nowhere to park close enough to the water to launch the boat. We ended up parking in the marina parking lot among the empty boat trailers and decided to get out and walk around to see if we could find another way out there.

The sidewalks were crowded with throngs of tourists, all in a hurry to get somewhere. Scores of gift shops lined the streets, and vendors were calling to passersby to come on in and see what they had to offer. We walked through several shops and enjoyed the chaos of Cabo.

The harbor was full of small open-bow boats zipping through the choppy water. We soon learned that these boats were water taxis that ferried people out to the peninsula to look at the attractions. Looking at the choppy water and hundreds of small boats' wakes crisscrossing the harbor, we were glad that we didn't try to kayak out in the bay.

As we neared the jetty, we were accosted by the shouts of water taxi drivers as they attempted to attract tourists to their particular boat. We quickly decided that it would be fun to take a water taxi and paid the ten-dollar per person fee and jumped in the boat. It took us about ten minutes to get out toward the arch, and our taxi driver/tour guide gave us a running commentary on all we were seeing.

The arch was cool to see up close and we took a bunch of pictures. We then continued on out a little farther till we reached Land's End. Land's End is the lonely little rock that marks the most southern tip of the Baja Peninsula. The waves crashed against it as we circled around, thus completing our journey, top to bottom, of the Baja Peninsula. We had done it!

The awesome thing about reaching our goal was the fact that even though our journey was complete, in a way we were still only halfway done, because we now had to travel the full length back up the peninsula to get home.

The driver then turned the boat around and drove us back toward Lover's Beach. Lover's Beach is a narrow patch of sand near the tip of the peninsula and is unique because it separates the Pacific Ocean and the Sea of Cortez. The two bodies of water are only separated by a hundred yards of sand. It's possible to play in the Pacific Ocean and then walk to the other side of the beach and swim in the Sea of Cortez in a matter of minutes.

The driver dropped us off in the surf and said he would be back to pick us up in about half an hour. It was fun to walk across the beach and get a glimpse of the Pacific Ocean. The surf was much stronger on the Pacific side, and the waves pounded the rocks and beach. We were able to take a picture of the Pacific side, turn around, and snap a picture of the Sea of Cortez without taking a step.

I tried snorkeling, but the swell was too rough and I didn't want to get smashed up on the rocks. Instead we sat on the beach and watched the constant stream of water taxis dump their passengers on the beach while others moved in close to retrieve theirs. When we got dropped off the taxi driver reminded us to remember the name of the boat, which I promptly forgot. I vaguely remembered a blue canopy and hoped I would recognize the boat when it returned. As promised the water taxi returned to collect us, and I recognized the driver as we waded out into the surf to meet him. It was a short ride and we were soon back on the dock. We walked back to the truck and decided that Cabo San Lucas was fun but a bit too touristy for us.

Just walking around Cabo, I could feel the flow of dollars from American wallets to Mexican pockets. In the short time we had been there, we had already parted with much more money than we had wanted to. Everyone seems to be selling something or wanting a tip for their services. Out on Lover's Beach there were several young men who waded out into the surf to help tourists unload and board the water taxis. For their effort they wanted at least a couple of dollars from each tourist. Judging from the number of people coming and going, I figured these guys were making at least twenty dollars an hour. Back in town there were signs everywhere advertising some type of product or service that catered to the American tourist. On the dock there was a Cabo San Lucas Fire Department stand selling fire department shirts. I parted with fifteen dollars and acquired myself a new T-shirt. The temptations are endless. If you stay for too long in Cabo, you will soon find your wallet empty.

Threading our way through crowded streets, we searched for Highway 19. Highway 19 leaves Cabo San Lucas and heads northwest up the Pacific coast, eventually making a big loop taking you back to Highway 1 near La Paz. We left Cabo San Lucas in our rearview mirror and headed north for the first time in over a week.

Our plan was to find a camping spot along the coast before reaching the town of Todos Santos. We were making good time and enjoying the views of the Pacific Ocean and ended up driving right past our camping spot and into Todos Santos. We pulled over, looked at the map again, and said, "Hey we're in Todos Santos," so we turned around to find the turnoff we had missed. Backtracking about ten miles, we found the turnoff and made our way to camp. The road had several sandy spots that made me a little nervous, but I gunned it and we sailed across no problem. We backed the truck in between two grassy sand dunes and set up camp.

The first thing we noticed about the Pacific side was the powerful surf. On the Sea of Cortez the water had been quite calm, with only small breakers about a foot high. Over on the Pacific side, huge sets of waves rolled in, one after another, and crashed on the beach. The average wave seemed to be at least four feet tall.

Out in the water we could see a group of surfers bobbing on top of their boards, waiting for the perfect wave. Other than their small surf camp set up at the far end of the beach, we were alone.

We lie on the beach reading our books and watching the surfers as the sun sank lower and lower. It felt nice to unwind and relax in solitude after a hectic day in the land of the tourist.

We dined on cup-o-noodles as the sun set over the rocky point at the far end of the beach. The sky was on fire with warm oranges and brilliant yellows bursting from behind the cold dark rocks. We sat in our camp chairs conversing about what an epic journey it had been so far. The trip had already exceeded most of our expectations. Each day had been packed with new and exciting discoveries. It was a bittersweet experience to have reached our goal so soon. Now that we had reached our goal, it meant that we would have to point the compass northward and embark on the trek back home. Kat reminded me that even though we were heading home, we still had almost a week left, and there would be plenty of exploring yet to do.

Map of Days 10 and 11

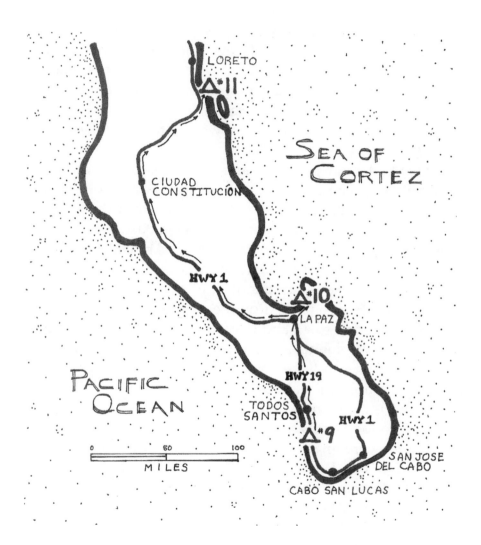

LORETO

△ #11
10

SEA OF
CORTEZ

CIUDAD
CONSTITUCIÓN

HWY 1

△ #10
LA PAZ

PACIFIC
OCEAN

HWY 19

TODOS
SANTOS

HWY 1

△ #9

0   50   100

MILES

SAN JOSE
DEL CABO

CABO SAN LUCAS

Day 10

Several drops of water splashed on my forehead, awakening me from a deep sleep. The rumble of heavy surf reminded me where I was, and I rolled over and opened my eyes. Everything was damp with the early morning dew. Condensation had collected on the underside of the kayak and was now raining down on us. Even my beloved pillow was wet. (I hate it when my pillow gets wet.)

A lemon yellow sun was rising over the mountains behind us, and its rays felt warm on our skin. We hung our bedding over a prickly bush to dry in the rising sunshine and prepared some breakfast. We waited awhile for our bedding to dry, but after breakfast it was still damp so we just packed it up wet.

It only took us about fifteen minutes to reach Todos Santos. We parked on the main street and got out to see what this town had to offer. A couple of blocks up the street we found a laundromat and decided that it would be nice to have some clean clothes. This gave us plenty of time to walk around Todos Santos while we waited for the laundry to finish.

Todos Santos is actually a very charming place, and we were glad that we had the time to wander around a bit. While wandering around the town we found a bunch of art galleries, cute little restaurants, and bed-and-breakfast type places. Many of these places were unassuming from the outside, but most had beautiful patio gardens and tasteful interior furnishings. The art community seemed to be thriving, with many studios and galleries open to the public.

We passed a quaint adobe coffee house with a grape arbor covering its patio area out front. Walking by we heard a mix of Spanish, French, and English being spoken, and I saw that several of the patrons had their laptop computers open as they drank their morning coffee. Todos Santos was surprisingly metropolitan for such a sleepy little town near the tip of the Baja Peninsula.

Another fun attraction in Todos Santos is the Hotel California. There is some doubt whether or not it is the actual Hotel California mentioned in the famous Eagles song, but it is a cute hotel and worth a visit. We ended up buying a neat antique map of Baja from their gift shop.

Ready to take a break from our morning stroll, we wandered over to the park to take a rest. The park was small and had many large shade trees that cast long shadows over the dusty grass. On one side of the park, bright yellow and green slides were set into the hill. Kat was fascinated to find out upon closer inspection that the slides and other playground equipment were made of poured concrete. She did a quick test on the slide and concluded that it worked just fine. Near the center of the park sat a small amphitheater and stage—a testament to the city's commitment to the arts.

After walking around Todos Santos for a morning, Kat and I decided that if we were wealthy, this would be the town to live in. Its close proximity to both Cabo San Lucas and La Paz coupled with its pleasant climate and artsy charm would make it an ideal spot to live.

We checked out some real estate flyers in the window of the local real estate office and realized that it would be quite a while before we purchased our second home here in Todos Santos. A two-bedroom, two-bathroom house located on the beach several miles from town was listed for 240,000 dollars—American. Granted, it was furnished and looked very nice, but it surely wasn't in our price range.

Tired of walking around, we headed to the grocery store near the laundromat, bought a two-liter bottle of Fanta, and sat out on the curb to enjoy it. This seemingly innocent act changed the rest of the trip for us. It was the start of a soda addiction that lasted the rest of the trip. I have been told that it is the sugarcane used in Mexican soda that makes it so good, but whatever the reason, we were hooked.

Almost every afternoon for the rest of the trip, we stopped after lunch at a small roadside store, plunked down our ten or fifteen pesos, and picked up a two-liter bottle of soda. Sometimes it would be Fanta Naranja, or Fanta Uva, or just regular Coca Cola. It didn't matter—they were all good.

We would then take turns drinking right from the bottle all afternoon as we drove until the bottle was gone. As the last few drops were guzzled, we would sadly look at each other and say, "You drank the whole bottle of soda." It was such a simple pleasure and helped the long afternoons in the car pass by quickly.

Once our Fanta was gone, we walked back to the laundromat to retrieve our laundry. With a huge bundle of sweet smelling clean clothes we headed back to the truck and drove northward out of town. After ten days on the road, we were very excited about the prospect of clean clothes.

About an hour later we neared the outskirts of La Paz. This time our drive through town was a bit more stressful due to increased traffic. Mexican drivers are very unpredictable in their driving habits. They seem to pick and choose at random which traffic laws to follow. You never know what is going to happen at a four-way stop sign, which is one of the primary ways intersections are controlled in Baja. Some drivers will ignore the stop sign completely and just drive right on through, others will do a stop and roll maneuver, while some actually come to a complete stop. The one thing that never varies at the four-way stop is that everyone feels it is their turn to go through the intersection first. All these factors made for some close calls and stressful driving.

Somehow we made it through the traffic and congestion of downtown without mishap. Thanking our lucky stars, we were happy to find ourselves in more familiar and safer surroundings along the waterfront. We decided that it would be nice to head out to the beach again.

We took the same road out past the ferry and Pemex refinery. The refinery was belching out a cloud of grey soot, and a large oil tanker stretched thick serpentine hoses across the water, either loading or off-loading petroleum products. The translucent rainbow swirl of film floating on the water around the tanker made me wonder if there were such things as environmental laws in Baja. From what we had seen so far, I guessed that if they existed they were probably more of a suggestion than an actual law.

The beach where we had previously snorkeled was so nice that we decided to return again. It was a bit more crowded today with the parking lot about half full.

We later figured out that it was the Saturday of Memorial Day weekend, which explained why there were a few more people out and about. The snorkeling was okay, but the wind and heavy swell of the past few days had made the water a little cloudy. We soon tired of the snorkeling since it was just so-so.

We kayaked over to our own beach on the far side of the cove to get some privacy. We frolicked and lazed about in the shallow warm water and soaked up the sun for a while. Kat found a little puffer fish floating belly up near shore and played with it for a while before giving it a proper burial at sea. The midday sun was fierce, and we were both starting to get a little sunburnt. By now our tans were looking pretty dark, and we didn't want to risk having it peel off after a bad burn.

The sun was getting high in the sky, and we figured that we had better get moving along. Paddling back across the clear water of the lagoon and looking back at the brilliant white sand made us realize what a prime spot we had found.

On the way out of town we stopped at the Pemex, filled up with gas, and said goodbye to La Paz as we turned onto Highway 1. It was already late afternoon, and we were hoping to camp near Loreto, so I drove fast and tried to make up time.

These long afternoons on the road gave us time to talk and relax. Many times Kat would have the map and guidebooks out in her lap and would read me tidbits of information. Together we would try to plan where to spend the night and figure out what there was to do in the area. With our flexible itinerary, there was always opportunity to discuss and explore all of our options before deciding where to camp or what to do the next day.

There is a certain freedom to being on the road. Anyone who has driven for days on end will attest to this fact. There's a certain sense of control over one's destiny that sometimes gets lost in our everyday lives. The only thing you have to do is stop every couple of hundred miles for gas. Other than that, it's your call. The thin ribbon of asphalt stretches over the horizon, and only the map in your hand can dictate where you can go. It was exciting to wake up each morning and not be certain exactly where we would end up.

When we had passed through Ciudad Constitución the first time on the way down, I had been napping and was now surprised to see what the town had done to control the highway traffic that passed through town. To help local traffic negotiate the highway, they have added additional lanes paralleling either side of the highway. These lanes on either side of the highway are one-way and are separated by a concrete barrier that has breaks in it every couple hundred feet to allow cars access on and off the highway. In addition to being one-way streets, these smaller lanes have very large speed bumps to control speed.

So to get off the highway we had to wait for a break in the barrier, turn onto the one-way street, and hope that it was going the direction that we needed to go. If we wanted to get to a store on the far side of the highway, we had to cross back over both lanes of traffic on the highway, while avoiding the oncoming traffic on the other one-way street. (If this sounds confusing, imagine trying to navigate this mess in your car.)

This system of traffic control made for some interesting driving conditions, as one can imagine. Cars would enter the highway going only a few miles per hour and then try to cross both lanes, while avoiding the local traffic on the one-way street. Once again, we suspected that this design must have looked much better on paper than it turned out to be in real life.

We hit Ciudad Constitución around dinnertime and figured it would be a good spot to find something to eat. After a few close calls trying to exit the highway and get to where we wanted to be, we found a roadside stand that had shaded outdoor dining and pulled down a dusty side road to park. We locked up the truck and walked over to do a closer inspection. It looked fine, so we walked up to the counter and ordered. The food turned out to be not only acceptable, but also cheap, with dinner only costing us 110 pesos. We had great seats right by the road, and it was fun to watch the traffic go by and all of the near accidents that occurred at an alarming rate.

There were several groups of old men sitting around us who were obviously local, and their familiar manner indicated that they frequented the restaurant. They sat around plastic picnic tables reading the paper, chatting, joking, and sipping drinks. It was fun to watch them in their element, and we lamented that it is getting harder and harder to find a local place to congregate where we live. The demands of busy schedules and increasingly hectic lives make it hard to find time to just relax and socialize with friends in the neighborhood.

After finishing dinner I cautiously made my way back onto the highway. It was touch and go for a few seconds until we got back onto the highway proper and put the pedal to the metal at the edge of town. It was late in the day, and I wanted to cover as many miles as possible before the sun set. We decided to camp at Playa Juancalito, where we had spent a night on the way down. It was nice to know in advance that we would find a good camping spot, since it was growing late and we didn't want to have to find a new spot in the dark.

We pulled into camp as the final twilight was fading. Once again, we had the place to ourselves. The moon was bright on the water while we set up camp and all was quiet. It had been a long afternoon with all the driving, and we were looking forward to sleeping in late and taking it easier the next day.

Day 11

When we awoke the sunshine was dancing on the water, illuminating the crests of the small breakers as they rolled onto shore. We lay in our sleeping bags soaking up the sun, in no hurry to get out of bed. It was beautiful: no alarm clock, no schedule to keep, nowhere to be — free from all external pressures and interferences.

While still in bed we pulled out the map and made plans for the day. Eventually the sun drove us out of bed and we retreated to the shade of a large palm tree. We ate a simple breakfast of instant oatmeal and went through the morning ritual of breaking camp and repacking the truck.

Our first destination for the day was Puerto Escondido. During our previous stay in the area, we had paddled by the harbor and quickly looked over the breakwater, admiring the sailboats. Today we were going to actually drive into the marina area and get out to take a closer look around.

Pulling into a large parking area near the water, we left the truck and got out to look around on foot. It was fun to see the sailboats and walk around the harbor area. Yachties puttered around the harbor in their zodiacs, calling greetings to each other and ferrying supplies to and from their boats. I was envious of their deep tans, nomadic lifestyle, and shared camaraderie.

The marina buildings, docks, and concrete pier were all in various stages of completion and disrepair. As we traveled across Baja, we noticed that many building projects seemed to get off to a strong start, only to flounder and remain half-finished and eventually be abandoned completely. Even in its less than ideal condition, the harbor was full of sailboats and busy with the hustle and bustle of sailors coming and going.

We walked out onto the crumbling concrete pier and took a closer look at a large fishing boat tied up at the dock. It was probably seventy feet long and looked like it had weathered many a storm. After looky-looing around the fishing boat, we went out to the end of the pier and admired the schools of fish and starfish that congregated around the support posts.

Leaving the marina, we only drove a couple hundred yards north on the highway before making a sharp turn onto a small dirt road that ran along some power lines. We followed the power lines until they ended at the mouth of a narrow canyon. There were several outbuildings and a transformer station near a low concrete flood dam that corralled a dry creek bed as it exited the canyon.

We parked in a patch of sagebrush and put together a day pack for the hike. This particular hike came highly recommended in one of the guidebooks, and we wanted to check it out. The book described a beautiful canyon hike complete with swimming holes along the way and spectacular ocean views from the top.

There must be a wet season when there is more water flowing in the canyon, because all we found were several shallow pools covered in fluorescent green pond scum. Even without the promised swimming holes, it was an awesome hike. There wasn't much of a trail, so we followed the dry creek bed up the canyon. At times we had to clamber over huge piles of boulders that were all jumbled together and blocked the way. In spots the canyon floor was so narrow that we had to climb up water carved channels and spouts in the bedrock.

We kept going up the canyon until we were blocked by house-sized boulders and sheer canyon walls. I looked for a way that we could climb over them, but I couldn't find a good route. Not wanting to give up quite yet, I attempted several routes but was unsuccessful. In the end we decided that it would be better to just stop here and enjoy the canyon before I hurt myself.

Once we decided that we could go no farther, we sat in the cool shade of the canyon walls and lounged on the smooth rocks. There was a brackish pool of water at the base of the rock pile where a waterfall had carved out a deep pothole. I thought about swimming but decided against it after noticing all the skeeter bugs and the thick layer of scum on the top.

Instead we lay on our backs, looked up at the canyon rim, and relaxed for a while. At first the soft music of the desert was inaudible until we sat quietly and let our ears grow accustomed to the sounds of the canyon. The call of desert wrens echoed softly in the canyon, and the sweet smell of sage hung in the air. We could hear the gurgle of water as it trickled down the sandstone and the rustle of the cottonwood trees as they swayed in the breeze. It was nice to pause for a few minutes and let ourselves get in tune with nature and feel the rhythms of the canyon.

There is something special about being in a canyon. Maybe it's the smooth sandstone that is so beautifully sculpted by the wind and water or the bright greens of the cottonwoods that surprise and delight the eye. Maybe it's the protection from the harsh sun and wide-open spaces of the desert that the narrow walls provide. Or it may just be the anticipation of discovering what is around the next bend. Whatever the reason, the solitude and grandeur found between the narrow walls speak to and soothe the soul.

As we walked down the canyon we could see the deep blue of the ocean only several miles away on the horizon. It was such a crazy contrast to be so close to the ocean, yet find ourselves deep in a desert canyon. Toward the end of the hike the noonday sun finally reached the depths of the canyon and the temperature instantly soared. Sweaty but stoked about the hike, we reached the truck and made our way back to the highway.

Heading up the coast along the bay, we made another quick side trip to visit the tourist development of Nopoló. This area is just south of Loreto and was slated for development into a mega resort in the late 1970s by Fonatur. Fonatur is the Mexican Government's tourism development agency and is in charge of increasing tourism in Mexico. In their quest to increase tourism in Baja, Fonatur has invested millions of pesos in several tourist destination areas.

Some of their developments have been very successful, while others have never caught on. Cabo San Lucas, Cabo San Jose, and La Paz are areas that Fonatur had great success with in the late 1970s. Nopoló was one of the places that didn't flourish. Actually, that is an understatement — Nopoló was a complete flop.

The development has a grand entrance with large gates and manicured gardens. There are wide boulevards lined with palm trees, expansive green lawns complete with sprinkler systems, and road signs written in both Spanish and English. We passed a large tourist welcome office, a golf course, and several parks. The streets are laid out in a neat and tidy grid, but the majority of the development's land sits fallow.

In spite of the beautifully kept grounds, the most obvious thing we noticed was the lack of houses, hotels, stores, and most importantly people. There are only a few streets with houses, and there are probably just as many half-finished and abandoned houses as there are completed ones. As we drove deeper into the development, we finally found a hotel at the far end, but the parking lot was mostly empty. The only people we saw the whole time while touring Nopoló were some hotel employees driving around in a golf cart.

Nopoló has a wonderful location with fine beaches and great views of Loreto Bay, but for whatever reason it never caught on or attracted foreign investors. It's almost like something out of the movie *Field of Dreams*—an elaborate tourist destination built out in the middle of nowhere, with the hope that if it is built, "they will come." Unfortunately for Fonatur, no one did.

It is unlikely that Nopoló will become the next Cabo San Lucas owing to the fact that the international airport constructed for the resort area has virtually closed down. The one airline that flies into the airport has almost ceased flights and thus sealed the fate of this development. Maybe someday it will receive more funding from Fonatur or private investors will breathe life into the project, but until then Nopoló will remain nothing more than a bureaucrat's pipe dream.

The plan was to continue up the coast and camp along the shores of Bahía Concepción again. We pulled into camp a couple of hours after lunch. Instead of camping at Playa Coco as we had done before, we decided to find a new spot along the shores of Bahía Concepción, preferably a little farther away from the highway and the roar of engine brakes.

We found a little out-of-the-way campground that had nice beach palapas and huts. The main draw to this camp was the large hill separating us from the highway. The downside was that there were several other groups camped in the campground and we had to pay for camping. We had been spoiled for most of the trip, and even one or two other campers made the beach feel crowded, but we figured it was a good trade-off to not be awakened during the night by semi trucks.

The afternoon was still young, so we changed into swimsuits and made a beeline for the warm water. Kat remembered that we had brought our floaty mats, and we pulled them out for the first time during the trip. (Floaty mats are inflatable pool mats used for floating around the pool and sunbathing—for those of you who maybe didn't know.)

We floated and played in the warm water for most of the afternoon. We would paddle out past the small breakers and then let ourselves be pushed ashore by the wave action of the water. Once we washed up on shore we would paddle back out and start all over again. While floating around Kat got the brilliant idea that we could use the floaty mats while we snorkeled.

We had to paddle the kayak out to a nearby island to try this revolutionary idea because of the thick seaweed near shore. Out on the island we beached the kayak, re-inflated the floaty mats, slipped on our masks and snorkels, and tried the first ever floaty mat snorkel expedition.

We found that it worked best to lie on the floaty mat face down with the upper body hanging off the top, putting our faces in the water and paddling with our hands. Floaty mat snorkeling was a huge success and turned out to be a very relaxing way to see the marine life below us. It also worked great in very shallow water, because we didn't get smashed on the sharp rocks below and could see everything very close up. I could feel my shoulder blades starting to burn after a while, so I got out and lay on the beach to burn my front side as well.

While lying on the sand I noticed a group of vultures eating something on the other side of the small beach, so I went over to investigate. It was a small sea turtle, only a few feet long. The poor little guy didn't make it. I would have loved to see one alive out in the water, but I hadn't had any luck yet. Kat wasn't interested in seeing the dead turtle, so we deflated the floaty mats and paddled back to camp.

The afternoon winds were picking up, and we rode the wind swells back to shore. It got a little crazy toward the end and we almost tipped over landing, but we made it without any disasters. Feeling the power of the wind and waves made me think that it might be fun to try surfing the kayak in the swell.

After dropping Kat off on the beach, I went back out in the kayak to play in the waves for a while. I tipped over immediately as I tried to surf my first wave and washed back to the beach. Undeterred, I tried it a few more times and continued to get worked in the surf. I was a having a good time, but the waves were only a foot or two high and not quite big enough to surf in on, so I dragged the kayak back up the beach. We spent the rest of the afternoon hanging out on the beach and relaxing.

As evening approached I decided to get the journal writing out of the way early. This seemed like a good idea, but I soon found myself

engulfed in a cloud of flies. They had been a little bothersome all afternoon, but something about writing in the journal got them really excited. They swarmed around my head and made it very difficult to write because I was constantly swatting at them. I stuck with it as long as I could but eventually had to stop for a while to concentrate fully on fly swatting. Kat tried to read her book but also had her own personal swarm of flies arrive. With the flies now bothering both of us, we decided that it would be a nice time to take a walk down the beach. This tactic worked pretty well to rid ourselves of the flies, and we enjoyed a nice sunset stroll.

After dinner we sat on the beach talking about what a cool trip it had been so far. We laughed at getting stuck in the sand the first night and were amazed at how long ago it seemed. Each day had been packed with new and exciting things to see and do. Almost half the pages in the journal were full of our adventures, and we still had almost a thousand miles to go. I was excited to explore more of the Pacific side and see new territory. The last few days had been great, but I was ready to see something new and break away from the path we had taken on the way down.

Sitting close to the water in our camp chairs, we had a long discussion about how glad we were to have this opportunity to see the *real* Baja—cactus filled desert, hostile dirt roads, empty beaches, clear warm water, and rugged mountain canyons. We felt privileged to experience the raw natural beauty that Baja has to offer to those who are willing to take the time to see it.

One thing that makes Baja so special is its accessibility. There is no need to board a plane, own all sorts of special equipment, or take out a loan to make the journey south. All you need is a reasonably sturdy car, gas money, some basic camping gear, and two or three weeks off work.

Of course, a little bit of bravado, determination, and dumb luck are also helpful. It is one of the few places left on the North American continent that offers such a wild and remote area in which to explore and recreate.

Map of Days 12 and 13

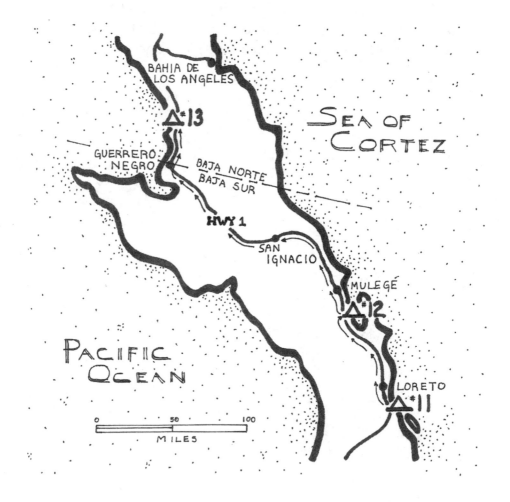

BAHIA DE
LOS ANGELES

△ #13

SEA OF
CORTEZ

GUERRERO
NEGRO

BAJA NORTE
BAJA SUR

HWY 1

SAN
IGNACIO

MULEGÉ

△ #12

PACIFIC
OCEAN

LORETO

△ #11

0   50   100

MILES

The buzz of flying insects around my head roused me from deep sleep, but it was the painful bite on my neck that really woke me up. The flies were everywhere—big, nasty, biting sand flies. Apparently they are early risers and wake up with an appetite. We were literally chased out of camp by hordes of flies as the sun rose over the water. It's funny because people always associate bugs with places like Alaska, but we encountered way more flying insects in our campsites on the beaches of Baja then we ever did up in Alaska.

This campsite turned out to be nice and quiet during the night, and we were glad that we had moved farther from the highway. Still, it was a relief to slam the truck doors and escape the flies as we drove away.

We stopped in Mulegé, hoping to use the Internet, but the shop was still closed owing to the early hour. Instead of waiting around, we decided to press on and try to find a place to use the Internet later in the day.

It wasn't long before we reached Santa Rosalíta. One of the guidebooks recommended a bakery in town, so we stopped to check it out. The bakery was excellent, and we were glad we stopped. The shop had a large glass counter with all sorts of breads and pastries displayed. Behind the counter was a large sign with all the different types of breads and pastries along with their prices. The individual baskets and trays of baked goods weren't labeled, so we had no way of knowing what was what or how much it cost. To overcome this dilemma, we simply decided to shop using the "pointing method." This method of shopping is simple: all you do is point at what you want and smile. Since this transaction didn't require any Spanish speaking, Kat took over the shopping duties and pointed to a whole bunch of different items that looked good. We soon ended up with a big bag full of goodies. It was fun to be able to shop and pick out exactly what we wanted without even knowing or caring what the price was. On our budget this doesn't happen very often, so we savored the moment, however small it was. Even utilizing the "pointing method," we only spent about 60 pesos.

We walked around town for a few minutes while we ate our breakfast. The guidebooks don't have very many nice things to say about Santa Rosalíta, but we found it to be just as nice as any other town we visited. It was a bustling place and full of life, with lots of people going about their morning duties. One interesting place in Santa Rosalíta that is worth checking out is a church that is made entirely out of stamped sheet metal. What makes it especially interesting is that the designer and builder of the church was the same man who built the Eiffel Tower. We took a couple of pictures and then walked back to the truck.

Just north of Santa Rosalíta Highway 1 makes a turn toward the west, and we took our last glimpses of the Sea of Cortez while filling up the truck at the Pemex station. From this point Highway 1 runs along the Pacific Coast or in the central valley. It was sad to think that we would be leaving the Sea of Cortez behind for good, but exciting that we would soon be traveling through new territory.

As the tank was filling, I asked the attendant if there was somewhere in town to buy some fish. He said he didn't know and hollered over to one of the other attendants to ask him if he knew of anywhere. Suddenly this other guy who was filling up his car chimed in and said he had some fish he would sell me.

Not sure what to say, I just stood there as he pulled out a cooler from the trunk of his car and asked, "How much fish do you want?"

Warily I asked, "How much is the fish?"

"Seventy pesos per kilo," he replied. Once again I was unsure what fish should cost and didn't know if this was a good deal or if I was getting ripped off. I thought about it for a second or two and concluded that this was a super convenient way to purchase fish, so I might as well do it now.

"Maybe a kilo," I replied. He then reached into the cooler and pulled out a Ziploc bag full of frozen fish fillets. He assured me that they were caught only days ago and would be excellent eating. Kat sat watching the whole thing from inside the truck, amazed that I had just purchased a bunch of fresh fish while pumping the gas. I packed the fish into our cooler, and we pulled back out onto the highway heading north.

It only took us about an hour to reach San Ignacio. Driving down the narrow streets, we found an Internet place in the small plaza across from the church. Painted on the front of the building was a sign announcing whale watching tours, and then in smaller print in the corner: "Internet use."

When we first walked in there was no one around, so we knocked and announced our presence, but the place was empty. We stood around for several minutes looking at the photos of whales on the walls before the owner sauntered across the plaza with his morning coffee in hand. This Internet place doubled as the office of a tour company that took people to see the whales in the winter and the turtles in the summer.

While Kat logged on to the Internet, I talked with the guy in the office about driving out to Laguna San Ignacio to check out the sea turtles. He told me that there were plenty of turtles out in the bay right now but that the law required us to have a licensed guide accompany us. He also mentioned that the road going out to the bay was in poor condition and was over forty miles one way. The prospect of eighty miles of washboard and the chance of a run-in with La Policía made me hesitant to embark on this side trip. With this new information we decided that it would probably be best to forgo the turtle viewing side trip.

After Kat was done with the Internet we walked around the plaza for a few minutes. Most of the shops were just opening, even though it was already after eleven in the morning. When we walked into one small vegetable market to ask for limes, the little old lady behind the counter said, "Oh no, we haven't had limes for months." With a smile and a shake of her head, she went back to reading the newspaper, which was laid out on the counter. I'm sure she was thinking, "Silly gringos, don't they know that limes aren't ripe in April?" Things seemed to move at a much slower, more comfortable pace in San Ignacio.

While crossing the state border in Guerrero Negro, we had to show our Tourist Cards for the first time. I was actually kind of excited about that, because they cost us forty dollars and no one had even asked to see them yet. After crossing the border into Baja Norte, we decided to find somewhere to eat lunch in Guerrero Negro.

We first stopped at a little roadside stand, but they only had carne asada plates. Kat took a look around the place and decided that we had better eat somewhere else. When we asked where we could find tacos they directed us a block up to the taco truck.

Now I am a little hesitant to get tacos from a catering truck north of the border, and I had some serious reservations about doing it down here, but we walked over anyways to see what they had.

The truck was a large white catering truck with a sign out front advertising fish tacos. The truck's exterior was freshly washed, and when we peeked inside everything was organized and looked sanitary, so we decided that fish tacos from a truck might just be okay.

After placing our order we watched the guy actually wash his hands after handling our money, which convinced us that we had made a good decision to eat there. We watched him dip the chunks of fish in batter and drop them into a boiling vat of oil. Once they were golden brown and crispy, he pulled them out and wrapped them in warm corn and flour tortillas. He was talkative and asked us about our trip while preparing the tacos.

Near the front of the truck there was an expansive salsa bar with different types of sauces and condiments to customize our tacos. We took our heaping platter of tacos and filled them with different types of salsas. The tacos turned out to be excellent. They were plump and very tasty. In fact, they were far and away the best tacos we had eaten so far during the trip, and we were very pleased with our taco truck experience. So if you're ever in Guerrero Negro, make a point of looking for the white taco truck.

Back in Baja Norte, we immediately noticed the increased military presence and passed through several military checkpoints before reaching the small town of Rosarito. We even had to get out at one checkpoint while they poked around in the truck for a few minutes. I was actually a little excited that we were finally getting searched. It had been anticlimactic to have gone through so many checkpoints without even so much as a "Please open the door, sir, and step out of the vehicle." I'm not sure what I was hoping for, but the search wasn't very exciting, which was actually a good thing now that I think about it. They didn't find anything questionable, and we were back on our way after a few moments.

While I was driving Kat was busy studying the map, looking for a place to camp. She discovered a small road that split off from the highway and went out to the coast. This road follows the coastline until it reaches the fishing village of Santa Rosalillita, where another road makes its way back to the highway. The road appeared to make about a fifteen-mile loop before returning to Highway 1 and seemed like it would be a nice side trip. Only one guidebook made passing mention of the road, but we decided that it would be fun to try it out. Kat was especially excited to read that along this stretch of coast there was a beach known for the many sand dollars that wash up on the shore.

We counted the kilometer markers carefully and at the designated marker saw a rutted dirt track going west. The road was pretty burly, with deep ruts and many steep arroyos to cross, but we decided to give it a try anyway.

Soon the highway disappeared behind us and we were all alone. Off in the distance we could see the white crests of the waves over the rocky berm that separated the ocean from the sandy desert floor. A scrubby windswept plain extended as far as the eye could see in either direction up and down the coast. The book mentioned that this part of the coast was devoid of development, but this was truly desolate and empty. It was beautiful.

There was a strong onshore wind blowing, and the truck rocked side to side when the gusts hit us broadside. Once we reached the rocky shoreline, we stopped and got out to stretch our legs. The beach was comprised of baseball sized volcanic rocks, and big breakers crashed onto shore. We were showered with salty spray as the wind blew the tops of the waves off. Farther down the beach we found several U-shaped windbreaks. They were built by stacking rocks together to form walls about three feet high and were big enough to park a car in. It must have taken someone quite a while to construct them, which made us think that the wind must be pretty constant here.

We got back in the truck and continued up the coast looking for the sand dollar beach. The rocky beaches continued on for several more miles, and we started to think that maybe the book had it wrong. A short time later the rocks were gradually replaced by sand and we grew hopeful again. We found a break in the rocky berm and stopped again to check out the beach. Kat was thrilled to discover that the beach was littered with sand dollars. We decided to make camp and spend the rest of the afternoon on the beach.

One of the first priorities was sand dollar collecting. We spent the next hour running from sand dollar to sand dollar. Kat collected over seventy of the most desirable sand dollars, and with our pockets full we made our way back to the truck. Kat then spent the next hour or two carefully sorting, washing, and drying her sand dollars. In the meantime I got the kayak ready to go play in the surf.

The waves were plenty big, and I guessed that they would have more than enough power to surf me. Well, I was correct about the power of the waves. They had no problem picking me up and smashing me as they broke. I got worked out there.

Our kayak was definitely not designed for this type of activity and had the tendency to try to turn itself sideways as I paddled down the face of a wave. The turning action of the kayak resulted in me getting rolled over as the wave crashed down on top of me. Once in a while I managed to hold the kayak straight and rode the wave for about two seconds before the nose dug into the bottom of the wave and I went end over end. I think I lucked out once or twice and actually surfed the wave all the way into shore without mishap. It must have looked like I was having fun, because Kat wanted to try it after I came back in. She had similar results, but we both agreed it was a fun time anyway. After tiring of the kayak, we shed our swimsuits and bodysurfed naked. We didn't see another person or car all afternoon and had the whole stretch of deserted coast to ourselves.

Back at camp I constructed a wind shelter using the tarp and kayak rack. It worked okay and offered some protection. Kat's sand dollars had dried nicely in the sun, and she was busy admiring them. It was starting to get late, so I got some coals started in anticipation of grilling the fish fillets for dinner. Along with the fish we had some grilled squash. I got the coals good and hot and the fish turned a crusty golden brown. Dinner was fantastic.

We went out and walked along the beach after dinner. As the sun sank lower over the water, the sky transformed from clear blue to mellow orange. Soon the sun kissed the water, backlighting the crashing surf and throwing reds and purples onto the glistening sand. After the sun had disappeared over the horizon, it immediately started to get colder. The temperature continued to drop as we walked back to camp, making it the coldest night so far on the trip. After being in the tropics for a week or so, we had definitely been spoiled. It was probably only sixty degrees, but it sure felt cold to us.

The wind was damp and my sleeping bag and pillow were clammy and cold as I got ready for bed. I hated that tons. Still grumbling about my wet pillow, I hunkered down into my sleeping bag, and we read our books for a while before turning off our headlamps. The stars were brilliant and sparkled across the blanket of darkness spread out above us. It had been a great day of discovery, and we were stoked to have stumbled upon this desolate and beautiful stretch of coast.

Day 13

My pillow was still wet in the morning when I woke up. Man, I hate a wet pillow. The damp wind had howled all night but had calmed down now. I was surprised that we weren't wetter with it as humid as it was. Dark clouds sat on the horizon threatening to roll in and dump rain on us. The prospect of rain made me a little nervous, because the road was already pretty rough, and mud would make in nearly impassible for us. Throughout the morning I kept a wary eye on the clouds, but they ended up dissipating before they reached the coast.

The warmth of the sun felt nice as we lay in bed, still lazing about and thinking of getting up. Kat got up first and brought her sand dollar collection into the back of the truck to carefully package each one. She wrapped each sand dollar up in a paper towel and then carefully placed it in an empty Triscuit cracker box. During our walk the previous night while watching the sunset, Kat limited herself to selecting only ten more sand dollars, now bringing her grand total to eighty. Three cracker boxes later, the sand dollars were all ready for the trip back home.

The cracker boxes served a dual purpose: first, they offered crush protection, and secondly, they provided a covert way to bring them home in case customs prohibited them from being brought across the border. It turned out that the customs people at the border could care less about sand dollars, but one can never be too safe when transporting large quantities of sand dollars across an international border.

After a lazy morning we packed everything up and took one last walk up and down sand dollar beach. It really was a treat to have discovered this lonely piece of paradise and have it all to ourselves. We contemplated spending another day in the area but in the end decided to press on.

The road continued to be very rough, and we had to crawl along at a snail's pace. The upside was that we were able to enjoy the scenery and stop often to look around. The desert flora was plentiful, and we took the time to take lots of pictures of the different types of cactuses and other desert plants along the way. These were the first pictures we had taken of all the many desert plants we had seen during the trip, because we had been worried about filling our camera's memory cards and running out of space to take other pictures. It was a fun to stop and try to find the biggest or most impressive plant and then take its picture.

We also stopped every few miles to check out the beaches. At one beach we found several rusting lobster traps strewn about and abandoned. They were battered and looked as if some big surf had tossed them up onto the rock berm. There were also all sorts of other bits of flotsam washed up onto the rocks—empty bottles, bits of plastic, and chunks of Styrofoam.

Farther down the road, when we stopped again at another beach, we discovered several interesting rock formations. A small arch, only a foot high and several feet long, protruded out from the sand—evidence of the tide's power to carve its way through solid rock. We took a picture or two and continued along our way.

I was a little bit nervous as the road's condition deteriorated into two parallel ruts. I could tell that things were going to get rougher as the road headed into the dunes. The road would drop down one side of a dune and shoot up the other side, only to veer off into another rocky gully. A little voice inside my head kept reminding me that we hadn't seen another vehicle on this road in over a day, and I knew that getting stuck was not an option. It wasn't a very reassuring thought as we bounced over the rough road.

While sliding down the steep embankments into the washed out gullies, I knew that I would have to somehow make it up the other side. I was heavy on the gas and made sure we had lots of momentum when I hit the other side. We made it up every time, bouncing along with all the tires spinning. The truck's suspension got a work out, but it performed adequately and we managed to make it through the rough spots without getting stuck.

The road eventually started to veer away from the coast and leveled out as it made its way into the foothills. The color returned to my knuckles as I eased my grip on the steering wheel and let out a sigh of relief. I was now

feeling pretty good about making it through the rough
stuff without any problems when we rounded a corner
and saw the Hill. The road took an abrupt turn and
proceeded to go straight up the side of the mountain. The
road was pockmarked with large divots and crisscrossed
with mini-canyons eroded by the spring monsoons. I
slowed and then rolled to a stop, putting the truck into
park. We both stared at the Hill and got out to do a quick
recon to see if we could make it. As I walked the twenty
yards up the Hill, I mentally mapped out the route I
would take and formed a plan of attack.

Kat was also a little doubtful if the truck could
make it up the Hill, but we reasoned that if we lost
traction halfway up, we could always just back down
and try again or turn around. Kat decided that she would
watch the hill attempt from the sidelines, and I walked
back down to the truck alone. I gripped the wheel tightly,
muttered a quick prayer, and put the pedal to the metal. I
didn't want to spin the tires and lose traction going up
the hill, but I knew that I would need as much
momentum as possible if I was going to make it.

The truck lurched and bounced over the divots. I
heard the gas cans, BBQ, and water jugs go flying in the
back. The tires squealed in protest as they spun over
basketball sized boulders and groaned as they regained
traction in the firm dirt. The cloud of dust kicked up by
the spinning tires engulfed the rear end of the truck, but I
kept my foot on the gas and maintained my forward
progress. I was about three quarters of the way up now
and had a good chance of making it—only a few more
feet and I would be on top.

The truck slid to a stop on the loose gravel as I
crested the hill. Success! The smell of burnt rubber and

dust hung in the air, and the truck still swayed slightly as the suspension regained its equilibrium. I had made it. I wiped my sweaty hands on my shirt and savored the view from on top of the hill. It wasn't a graceful ascent, but I didn't care one bit.

It took a minute to rearrange the gas cans and other things that had flown around the back of the truck, but soon things were back where they should be. Kat walked up the hill, all smiles that I had made it. From our vantage point on top of the hill, we could see the little town of Santa Rosalillita a few miles up the coast.

Lobster traps were piled along side the road in great heaps as we entered Santa Rosalillita. This was a small village with only a smattering of small houses scattered along the bay. Judging by the lobster traps and fishing nets piled in the front yards of all the houses, just about everyone in town must gain their livelihood from the sea.

A few kids came out of their houses to stand alongside the road and stare at us. We waved and they shyly smiled and looked at their feet. I think our big yellow kayak was our main draw. We followed the road through town and found the turnoff that would lead us back to the highway. The road back to the highway was unpaved but had recently been graded and was in good condition.

After traveling a few miles toward the highway, all of a sudden the road widened and pavement abruptly began. It was by far the widest paved road we had seen in Baja. It would have accommodated at least four or five lanes. It was bizarre that out in the middle of nowhere, a spacious paved highway just appeared. I stopped to take a picture of the oddity and Kat looked in the guidebooks to see if they made mention of it.

It turns out that this was another brilliant Fonatur scheme. In the late 1980s Fonatur decided to construct a land bridge between Santa Rosalillita and Bahía de Los Angeles. A land bridge is a wide road that connects two ports and facilitates boats crossing overland on large trucks. This proposed land bridge would make it easier for pleasure boats to cross over from the Pacific Ocean into the Sea of Cortez, thus eliminating the need to go all the way down and around the tip of the peninsula. It seems like a pretty good idea, but for whatever reason construction has ceased. Santa Rosalillita remains a small underdeveloped fishing village, and only a few miles of the land bridge are completed. Fonatur has a projected completion date of 2014 for the land bridge, but at this time there seems to be little activity or progress being made. Although such a land bridge could be beneficial for Baja, it would be a shame to develop and change such a beautiful empty stretch of coastline.

Back on Highway 1 we drove through great forests of cardón cactuses. Their sheer numbers and the density in which they grew were amazing. Huge cactuses covered the hills as far as the eye could see—there must have been hundreds of thousands of them. I had never seen such a concentration of cactuses before in my life.

We soon arrived at the town of Cataviña and stopped to grab some lunch. There wasn't much selection, only one café, so we decided to eat there. We sat outside under the patio, facing the highway, and watched the traffic speed past us. A cute little puppy dog wandered over to our table and watched us eat with large mournful eyes. Kat couldn't resist feeding him bits of her lunch and soon had a lifelong friend. Lunch was tasty and a bargain at 100 pesos. Kat sadly said goodbye to the puppy and we hit the road. The scenery continued to be interesting with large rock outcroppings springing out of the sand and large arroyos cutting across the desert.

Our next destination was the ghost town of El Marmol. El Marmol is an old mining town, now abandoned, where onyx was quarried. The town and quarry are located about ten miles off the highway. Fortunately the road was in pretty good condition with minimal washboard.

Onyx is a stone similar looking to marble and was used extensively in the nineteenth century in the making of doorknobs, floor tiles, and other household items. At one time a small town of several hundred inhabitants flourished in the desert, complete with a school, jail, and cemetery. With the advent of plastics and the increased cost of mining, the demand soon dried up for onyx, and the quarry shut down in the mid 1950s. The quarry has sat unused for the most part since then, except for some small-scale mining by local artists who use the stone in their carvings.

The guidebooks said that El Marmol was an interesting side trip, and we were excited to check it out. Luckily the dirt road was in good condition, and we were able to make it out there fairly quickly. There isn't much left of the town—all that remains is the crumbling schoolhouse, a small cemetery, and a lonely row of foundations.

The quarry itself was fun to walk around, with huge chunks of onyx lying around and several dusty roads to explore. The onyx's coloring varied, but most pieces were different shades of orangey red with white, yellow, and cream colored swirls. Each rock had differing stratification and colorings that made it unique. The rock had a translucent quality, and the afternoon sun made the thinner pieces glow orange around the edges. We collected several small chunks of onyx that caught our fancy to add to our collection.

There were several pieces of heavy machinery left around the quarry, and I took Kat's picture while she pretended to drive a crane. After exploring the quarry we wandered back toward what was left of the town. The roof of the schoolhouse had long since rotted away, and only three walls were left standing. The walls were constructed of unpolished blocks of onyx and were at least two feet thick. There were several window openings cut in the walls and encased in heavy timbers. A rusty barbed wire fence surrounded the school—probably to keep out curious tourists. Undeterred, I climbed through the barbed wire fence to examine the inside of the schoolhouse. Up close I could see how the large blocks were cut to fit next to one another and carefully mortared together. I took several pictures in and around the schoolhouse as Kat reminded me that I really shouldn't be inside the fence.

The cemetery was overgrown and many of the headstones had fallen over. Mounds of crumbling onyx covered the graves and tall weeds poked through. The names were worn off the larger monuments, and several graves only had simple crosses without markings. We wandered around the cemetery but soon had to seek the shade of the only tree around to escape the harsh desert sun. After wandering around the town and quarry for the better part of an hour, we decided it was time to try to find the hot springs.

The guidebooks mentioned that there were several hot springs in the area and gave vague directions on how to find them, but the directions varied from book to book. On the far side of town there were several dirt roads to choose from, so we made an educated guess and picked the one that best fit the books' descriptions.

We followed the road for several miles, not wanting to turn around early and miss the hot springs over the next hill or around the next bend. The road was strewn with loose rock and required careful driving. As we climbed a large hill up onto the plateau, I noticed that I could do a complete 360 without seeing any signs of civilization. "Hmmm. . . This would be a really bad place to have a mechanical problem or get stuck," I thought. I imagined myself walking down a dusty dirt road, miles from anywhere, with the sun setting over my shoulder, looking for someone, anyone to help us. With this unsettling thought I made a mental note to be very careful and not take any foolish chances.

We continued to press on until a small cactus growing in the center of the road blocked our way. It was a prickly little guy about two feet tall with long spindly arms. There was an elephant tree and a bigger cactus on either side of the road, so I had no alternative but to drive over it. I was worried that it might hurt the truck, so I asked Kat jump out with our small shovel and see if she could flatten it down. Nothing doing—the cactus proved to be firmly rooted in the rocky soil and wouldn't budge. Not having any other alternatives, I was forced to slowly drive over it. It made a terrible noise scratching the bottom of the truck, but after running it over the cactus popped back up no worse for the wear. In my mind's eye I could see steam billowing out from under the hood as a hose ruptured, but after a quick inspection the truck's underside seemed unharmed. Disaster averted once again.

At one point the road took a sharp turn and began to descend steeply into a small box canyon. Not wanting to take any more chances, we decided it would be best to proceed on foot. The sun was scorching and heat radiated back up from the desert floor, hitting us squarely in the face. We plodded along, but soon the road petered out and there didn't seem to be any sort of trail. There were no signs of any hot spring in the area.

Discouraged, we turned around and climbed back up the road to the truck. I turned the ignition switch in the truck, and thankfully it fired right up after the first crank. With the air conditioning going full blast, we discussed what we should do next.

Looking out through the windshield, we could see that the sun was getting lower in the west and there were no signs of any hot springs. Concluding that you can't always find everything, we made the decision that it was time to turn around. I hate to give up, but sometimes it's best to cut your losses and move on.

It was still a fun trip out into the desert, and from on top of the plateau we could see for miles into the interior. It was beautiful in a dry and inhospitable way, but it definitely wouldn't have been a fun place to get stranded.

On the way back we repeated the cactus-running-over maneuver and managed to make it back to El Marmol without incident. Even though we didn't find the hot springs, the visit to El Marmol was fun and well worth the trip.

After turning back onto Highway 1, we saw a small sign advertising carved onyx figures. We turned off and pulled up in front of a small house with another sign indicating that this was indeed the onyx shop. The windows were dusty and there was no sign of life, so I jumped out to check it out while Kat waited in the car.

I knocked on the door and was greeted by an old man who motioned me inside. The front room had a long table that was filled with carvings of all sorts of animals. Hundreds of wind chimes made out of thin onyx pieces hung from the ceiling, chiming gently with the breeze that entered from the open front door. We exchanged greetings and I asked him the prices of various pieces. The prices that he quoted me were reasonable, so I told him that I would be right back.

I went out and got Kat, and we came in to look around. I started conversing with the guy in Spanish while Kat looked at the various carvings. When I asked him if the stone came from Marmol he answered, "Si," "these carvings are made from the onyx from El Marmol." He then went on to tell me how he had personally gotten the stone from the quarry and hand carved each piece. He told me that he worked in the quarry as a young man and remembered when they shut the operation down in the 50s.

Kat finally selected a large turtle weighing at least ten pounds, and I wanted to get a wind chime for my mom since mother's day was coming up. When I asked him how much, he replied, "For you, I will give you a good price." Even though this sounded vaguely familiar, I ignored the thought and pressed on. He told me that it could all be mine for four hundred pesos. I countered with two hundred and the price was agreed upon at three hundred. We stayed and chatted for a few minutes after the sale and left feeling happy about our "good price" and helping a local artist.

Later in the trip we saw many of the same onyx carvings and tried to tell ourselves that the old guy must have been very busy to carve enough figures to supply so many shops. You would have thought that we would have learned our lesson by now, but we hadn't. Regardless, it was fun to think that the turtle came from El Marmol, and once again we had a souvenir with a story.

With our turtle and wind chimes carefully wrapped in newspaper and packed away, we got back onto the highway. It was pretty late in the afternoon, and we needed to make some time so we could find a camp before dark.

The geography was changing rapidly. The desert plains grew into rolling hills, which in turn grew into great rounded mountains. The road twisted and climbed gradually up the mountainsides until it made its way to the ridgeline. The road continued to follow the crests and gave fantastic views of the valleys below.

As we got closer to the town of Rosario, the weather began to change. Puffy grey clouds cast shadows on the valley floor, and off in the distance we could see rain falling in grey sheets. As we drew even closer, darker pancake shaped clouds rolled over the mountaintops and several raindrops splattered on the windshield. I rolled down the window and could feel that the temperature had dropped. We certainly weren't in the tropics anymore. We gradually descended down the mountain, following sweeping switchbacks, and hit a wall of fog in the narrow valley below. The fog continued to swirl around us as we neared Rosario.

Rosario is a collection of brightly painted houses and festive looking restaurants nestled between two grassy mountains. Many of the restaurants had signs outside advertising seafood and lobster, and we had heard good things about the local cuisine. Had the weather been better we would have enjoyed getting something to eat, but the gloomy weather discouraged us from stopping.

We were ready to find somewhere to camp before the weather got really bad and started dumping rain. Our minds were made up, and I accelerated as we left the valley, rushing toward the coast.

The fog thinned out as we neared the coast again and sunbeams poked holes in the clouds, creating a patchwork of sunlit spots on the grassy hills. The sun brightened our mood, and we began to look for a spot to spend the night as we drove along. The guidebooks indicated that the nearest good camping spots were still miles up the highway, but we soon saw a bunch of dirt roads leaving the highway in the direction of the beach. It was getting late, and with the dwindling sunlight we decided to check one out and hopefully find a spot. There was a maze of dirt roads that crisscrossed through the dunes, and we weaved our way toward the beach while trying to avoid the sandier areas. We soon found ourselves on the edge of a tall bluff overlooking a rocky beach below.

Parking the truck, we got out to walk around the area and see what it had to offer. There was a steep winding path that led down to the beach below. We took a look, but decided that it was too rough to take the truck down.

It was cold and we had to put on our fleece jackets to ward off the chill. Even with our fleeces on, the stiff wind that was blowing up over the bluff cut right through and made us shiver. After scouting out the area, we decided that it would be fine to camp up on top of the bluff. We were about half a mile off the highway and could still see headlights, but it was relatively quiet and deserted, so we found a level spot and parked the truck.

I quickly got the coals started for dinner while Kat set up camp. It was nearly dark now, and I had to use my headlamp while cooking dinner. We finished up the fish, and for dessert Kat sliced up a fresh pineapple that we had purchased earlier in the day. It was sweet and reminded us of the tropics that we had left only a few days ago. As I sat bundled up in a fleece and long pants, I already missed the hot sunshine and warm breezes of

Baja Sur. The only advantage of the cooler weather was the lack of sand flies and other bugs around camp.

After cleaning up dinner, we dragged our camp chairs over near the edge of the bluff to watch the waves crash on the beach. The luminous white froth washed up on the rocks, marking the steady rhythm of the sea. Stormy clouds on the horizon were outlined in silver by the moonlight and drifted slowly as the wind pushed them across the sky. Kat read her book and snuggled close while I wrote in the journal. The wind and cold eventually drove us to bed early. Bundled up in our sleeping bags, we read our books and watched the clouds go sailing by overhead.

I was nearing the end of *Log from the Sea of Cortez* and was consciously trying to slow my reading down and savor what remained of the book. I would find myself reading too quickly and then make myself reread it at a slower pace to get the full enjoyment out of it.

As I struggled to make the book last as long as possible, it started to sink in that our Baja Adventure was also nearing its completion. It was a bittersweet thought that in only a few short days we would have to return to real life and leave Baja behind. It had been a marvelous trip, exceeding all our expectations, but even the most adventurous person among us eventually starts to feel the pull of home after a while. The thought of our snug little house and comforts of home were calling, and tempered my feeling of sadness that the trip would soon be over.

Map of Days 14, 15 and 16

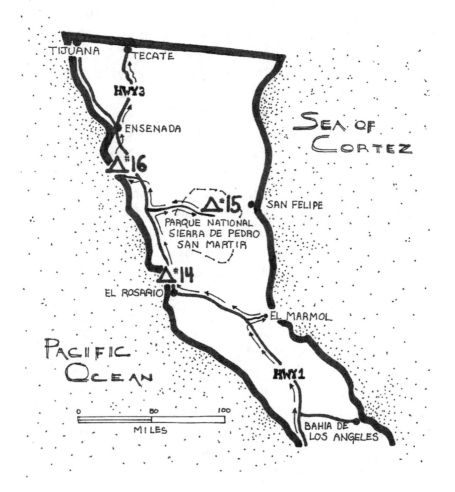

TIJUANA
TECATE
HWY3
ENSENADA
△#16
SEA OF CORTEZ
△#15 SAN FELIPE
PARQUE NATIONAL SIERRA DE PEDRO SAN MARTIR
△#14
EL ROSARIO
EL MARMOL
PACIFIC OCEAN
HWY1
0   50   100
MILES
BAHIA DE LOS ANGELES

Day 14

The growl of an overloaded pickup truck in low gear driving past our campsite awoke us in the morning. The sky was overcast and grey, but at least the wind had died down some. The driver and the five passengers in the back waved at us as they bounced their way down the deeply rutted bluff road toward the beach.

We sipped hot chocolate and sat sleepily around the camp stove, trying to fend off the early morning chill that hung in the air. My pillow was still damp, and I had a few choice words to say about that when I woke up. We were both feeling sticky and in need of a shower, but unfortunately the water in the sun shower was freezing cold after the long night.

Feeling ambitious, I started to boil pots of water to fill the shower, and soon we had enough hot water to take quick showers. The hot water felt so good, but it was hell when my turn was up and I had to dry off as quickly as possible. Changing into new clothes, I felt much more alive and ready to start the day.

We decided to take a walk along the bluff and see what the place had to offer in the daylight. Peering over the edge, we noticed that there were bunches of people down on the beach, hunched over, apparently collecting something in large burlap bags. Curious, we decided to walk down to the beach and see what they were up to.

Down on the beach we approached the pickup that had driven past us earlier. There were several guys standing around talking and drinking their morning coffee. I greeted them in Spanish and they invited us over. I could see several bulging burlap bags already loaded in the back of the truck and noticed that the suspension was already riding low under the weight. After introductions were made, I asked them what they were collecting. They replied that they were collecting the rounded beach stones to sell up north. When I pressed further, they said that the stones were used for landscaping and that gringos paid big bucks for them. With smiles, they asked me if I would like to buy some rocks for my yard at home. They said that they would give me a "good price" on a truckload of rocks.

Laughing, I declined their offer. I wished them luck in their rock gathering endeavor, and we continued walking down the beach. We passed another group loading up bags full of rocks into the large trunk of their beat-up Lincoln Town Car. The car's tail end was already almost touching the ground under the weight, but they continued to pile in more bags. About half of the gatherers were women and children, each filling their bag with stones. These hardworking people certainly make use of what limited resources they have available to them.

I could just imagine how different the situation would be north of the border if such a beach were found. The small-time rock gatherers would soon be put out of business as a wealthy entrepreneur moved in with heavy equipment and dump trucks. The natural resource would be depleted within several weeks. Soon all that would remain would be the scars of heavy machinery tracks across the dunes and the lingering stench of diesel fumes. It's ironic that the limitations of poverty and lack of capital sometimes do more to preserve the environment than any environmental laws or regulations. I'm sure that these rock collectors had been gathering rocks for years, but due to their small-scale operation they hadn't even put a dent in the beach's supply of rounded landscaping rocks.

After walking down the beach for a while, we turned around and headed back. We waved our goodbyes to the rock gatherers and climbed up the bluff to our camp. We packed everything up and got ready to leave. The plan for today was to continue our way north up past San Quentin and then turn east into the Sierra San Pedro Mártir Mountain range.

This mountain range runs down the center of Baja for hundreds of miles and separates the two coasts. The mountains are extremely high and form a barrier that prohibits the cool Pacific weather from crossing over to the more temperate eastern side of Baja. The tallest peak in Baja, Picacho del Diablo, sits on the eastern side of the mountain range and is 10,498 feet above sea level. We planned to visit the national park, or Parque National, that protects a large portion of this mountain range.

One of the main points of interest inside the Parque National is the National Astrological Observatory. This celestial research center has a powerful telescope and houses astronomers from around the world. The Parque National is quite remote and requires a sixty-mile one-way side trip to reach the entrance, so we wanted to spend at least a day or two in the park. With the day mapped out, we made our way back to the highway.

Highway 1 hugs the coastline as it progresses northward toward San Quintín. The highway was much busier, with lots of traffic going in both directions. The cars seemed to be older and more beat-up in this area, and subsequently some traveled at much slower speeds than we were accustomed to.

This made for some hairy driving, because there were also a significant number of cars on the road that wanted to travel much faster than the slow cars. Of course the highway was only two lanes and had lots of blind curves, but this didn't stop many cars from passing whenever they felt the need. Little regard was given to such things as visibility or the fact that oncoming traffic was approaching at breakneck speed. We witnessed several near head-on collisions and now understood why there were so many crosses and flowers alongside the highway.

The desert gradually gave way to cultivated farmland and the landscape was much greener. Workers toiled in the fields, bent over double harvesting the crops. The land seemed fertile and the fields seemed to sprout many different types of grains and vegetables.

We soon arrived in San Quintín and stopped to fill up with gas at the Pemex. Our water supply was running low, so we looked around for a place to buy purified water. We found a place that looked just like a convenience store north of the border, with a glass front and a clean white tile floor. I took in one of our five-gallon water jugs and started to use the self-serve water filling station inside the store.

I somehow got distracted or just wasn't paying close attention to the water level inside the jug, and before I could stop the water, the jug was overflowing onto the floor. To compound matters, my feet were dusty and my flip-flops had dried mud on them, so the growing puddle of water on the clean tile floor soon turned to mud. There I was standing in the middle of a huge mud puddle looking like an idiot. I was totally embarrassed and mumbled an apology to the two teenage girls working there.

Shamed, I grabbed the jug and paid for the water quickly, leaving a hefty tip. Unfortunately the jug was still full to the brim, and I ended up sloshing water on the floor all the way out the door, leaving a muddy trail across the white tile. It was definitely not one of my finest moments. I'm sure the girls just shook their heads and wondered how I had managed to make it this far into Baja.

A few miles north of town, we saw the small brown sign indicating the turn-off for Parque National Sierra San Pedro de Mártir. The road passes through the picturesque farming valley of San Telmo before it starts its ascent into the mountains. Craggy granite peaks dominate the eastern horizon and tower above the foothills. Large herds of cows grazed along the road, and we saw some real Mexican cowboys out on their horses.

The road through the valley is narrow, only one and a half lanes wide, but is paved and in good condition. The pavement continues as the road climbs up and over the foothills. It appears that the road will be paved all the way to the Parque National in the next few years. We saw lots of heavy machinery and a few road crews hard at work. It was evident that this was a large project that had been going on for some time.

Even after the pavement ended, the dirt road was a dream come true. It was freshly graded and very smooth. We waved to the road crews and tried not to get run over by the huge road graders as they lumbered along. We stopped every once and a while to get out and enjoy the views.

About halfway up the mountain we burst through the cloud cover into blue skies and sunshine. Up above the cloud cover the sun was shining brightly and we could see for miles. The valley floor was laid out before us, and fields of yellow wildflowers covered the foothills. It was possible to see all the way out to the Pacific Ocean.

The road continued to climb up the mountain, and the vegetation began to change as we gained elevation. Soon scrubby pine trees started appearing, which then transformed into a thick forest. The road conditions got a little rougher as we got closer to the park entrance, but overall it was an easy trip and only took about an hour and a half.

What made this particular road construction project so interesting was that fewer than five thousand people visit this park every year, which equates to probably fewer than two thousand cars. On the way up to the park we only saw two cars, and both looked like local ranchers. It seemed like a lot of resources, time, and money were being spent on a sparsely used section of road.

During our travels on the highways of Baja, we had seen many road crews working on different sections of the major highways—mostly repairing potholes and things like that. One thing that we noticed right away was that almost all the work was done with hand tools and pure manual labor. On one stretch of Highway 1 in Baja Sur, we saw a crew pouring large sections of a drainage ditch alongside the highway. They were mixing all the concrete by hand in five gallon buckets and then using wheelbarrows to pour it. But today we saw bulldozers, dump trucks, and graders all being used on this remote section of secondary road. The allocation of resources in Baja certainly is a mystery to us.

At the park's entrance there is a gate and a small A-frame building. The first thing we noticed when we pulled up was the snowdrift nestled against the A-frame. "Snow?" we both said in disbelief. The dirty snow was slushy and melting but was still several feet deep.

The mountain air was crisp and the smelled of pine. The sun shone brightly through the thin air and made us squint as we walked over to the A-frame. A single ranger greeted us, and we paid our seventy-peso admission to the park. In return we got a topo map of some remote area that wasn't even in the park boundaries, a flyer in English on the California condor (distributed by some group from San Diego), and a Xeroxed road map of the park's one road—completely out of scale. Classic Baja.

The ranger explained to us that he was the sole ranger on duty for the whole park and asked us to leave a note at the gate when we left so he would know that we made it out safely. With these instructions we got back in the truck and drove into the park.

Several miles into the park, we stopped at the Mirador trailhead. This hike winds up to the summit of a tall outcropping of granite that gives the hiker a view of the Pacific Ocean to the west and the Sea of Cortez to the east. The beginning of the trail was steep, and we soon noticed the high elevation as we sucked in great gulps of air and still couldn't catch our breath completely. It was a shock to our lungs to go from sea level to over nine thousand feet in just a matter of a couple of hours. The thin air tired us out quickly and we had to slow our pace. The trail eventually leveled off a bit, and soon we found ourselves walking through groves of Aspen trees. In the shadows small streams and rivulets of water ran off from the melting snowdrifts.

We soon reached the lookout point and were greeted with spectacular views in both directions. Off to the east we could see the blue of the Sea of Cortez, but it was too hazy in the west to see the Pacific. It was well worth the three-mile uphill hike, and we lounged about on the rocks soaking up the sun while enjoying the view.

We didn't see another hiker the whole time, and it was neat to have the place to ourselves. After eating our snacks and taking some pictures, we slowly made our way back down the trail. It was much easier descending, and we made it back in half the time. It was now getting later in the afternoon, so we decided it was time to look for a camp spot.

There were several designated camping areas marked on map, but the ranger had asked us to only use the one closest to the park's entrance. This was fine because so far we had only seen one other car inside the park and figured we wouldn't have to deal with any crowds. It turned out that we were correct. We didn't see anyone else all night.

We found a nice spot on the edge of a meadow that had a flat spot to park the truck and a granite boulder to use as a cooking table. Nestled under the pine trees, the temperature was already getting cooler even though we still had several hours of daylight. We both put on our fleeces and long pants and settled into making camp. We broke out our hammock for the first time and looked around for a place to string it up. We had a hard time finding two trees that were the proper distance apart and had to settle for two that might have been a little bit too close together. As I settled into the hammock my rear end touched the ground while my feet and head stayed nicely elevated. Not an ideal position for lounging, but it was still fun to take turns swinging each other in the hammock.

Hungry from our hike and day of driving, we cooked an early dinner. The kitchen rock worked out great and made the preparation and cooking very easy. Our food supplies were starting to run low, but we rummaged around and found some pasta and dried Italian salami. The food was tasty and warmed our tummies. After dinner we decided that it would be fun to take a quick exploratory hike around the campground and walk off our dinner.

The meadow was beautiful and we followed a small stream that wandered through it and listened to the croaking frogs. I wanted to try to catch a frog, but every time I got within ten feet of the water the croaking instantly ceased until I backed off. I tried to be as quiet and as sneaky as possible, but the frogs were too wary and I couldn't locate them once they stopped croaking.

Pale pinks and purples filtered through the trees as the sun sank lower over the forest. Hoping to see the sunset, we hurried to the edge of the meadow where it appeared that we could see out of the trees. The view was blocked by more trees, but once again it appeared that if we went just a little farther we could get a clearer view of the sunset. We scrambled over fallen logs and through the forest bramble hoping to get a view before the sun set completely. We never quite made it to the edge of the mountain to see out over the valley below, but we had a fun time chasing the sunset and got some pretty pictures with the trees silhouetted in a sea of pinks, purples, and yellows.

We made our way back to camp in the fading light, glad to have found our way without mishap after dashing so recklessly through the forest. The stars were sparkling brightly just above our heads by the time we reached camp.

Back in camp the temperature began to plummet. To ward off the chill we kept adding new layers of clothes until soon we were both wearing just about every article of clothing we had brought with us on the trip.

With the many layers of T-shirts, fleeces, vests, hats, and thermals, we both looked pleasantly plump and much rounder than normal.

We settled into our camp chairs and sipped hot chocolate as we marveled at the radical change of scenery. Just a few hours ago we had been walking along the beach, and we now found ourselves camping in a high alpine meadow. Baja was proving itself once again to be a land of extremes and full of surprises.

With the temperature now hovering in the low 40s, we contemplated building a campfire but had neglected to gather firewood while it was light. The forest was cold and dark and neither of us was excited to wander out into the woods in search of firewood. Instead we abandoned our chairs around the lantern and climbed into our sleeping bags. It was much warmer snuggled deep in our sleeping bags, and we talked about our plans for tomorrow.

Sunbeams warmed our faces as we slowly started to emerge from our cocoons. It had been a long cold night. I had kept reasonably warm, but Kat froze. The air was still and quiet. Camping on the beach for so long had made us accustomed to the crash of surf, the whistle of wind across the dunes, and the squawk of sea gulls. The crisp clean silence of the high mountain glade was overpowering.

Frosty blades of grass out in the meadow glistened as the sun moved toward us, transforming the ice crystals into glittering drops of dew. It was still pretty cold, but at least the frost was melting. We lounged about in our sleeping bags, basking in the sun and waking up slowly. It felt like we were the only ones around for miles, and we probably were.

After finishing up breakfast and packing the truck, we made our way back out to the main road. The observatory is located near the center of the park, and it took us about forty-five minutes to reach the turn-off. The turn-off was marked with a small sign indicating that this was the road that led to the National Observatory, with a smaller sign under it instructing visitors to check in with the supervisor. A little way up the dirt road we found the main administration building along with the housing for the astronomers. The housing units were funny looking buildings with rounded roofs, which made them look like igloos. Parked in the parking lot was a fleet of white Volkswagen Beetles with the National Observatory's symbol painted on the door.

Not really knowing where to find the supervisor, I parked and we got out to look around. There were several construction workers painting the exterior of what looked to be a new conference center. I strolled over and asked them where I could find the supervisor, and they said that he had been around earlier but had left. We then wandered toward a large maintenance shop where several snowplows were parked outside. There were a few mechanics working on dump trucks and other heavy machinery, but they didn't seem interested in our presence so we headed back to the car. Discouraged with finding a supervisor, I figured that we could drive farther up the road to the actual observatory and feign ignorance if we were confronted about entering without permission.

As we were getting back in the truck, a guy walked out of one of the dome shaped huts and started toward one of the Beetles. I got back out and started talking with him. He introduced himself as Juan Carlos. He said that he was an astronomer visiting the observatory to complete some research he was currently working on. He was friendly and told me about the observatory and how it was run by the University of

Mexico. When I asked him where everyone was, he said that since most of the observing is done at night, most of the astronomers sleep during the day so they can work at night.

We talked for a few minutes until the supervisor pulled up in his truck. Juan Carlos introduced me to Santiago, the supervisor. I inquired if we could take a tour of the observatory this morning, and he replied that we were in luck because he was expecting a high school class to arrive any moment for a tour and we could join with them. He told us to follow him, and then he jumped back into his truck and we sped off down the hill.

We met up with the school bus and formed a convoy. Santiago was very particular about having us follow right behind him and stick to the road. There must be lots of valuable scientific equipment around that has to be watched over carefully. It took us about half an hour to reach the top of the mountain.

The observatory stands on a rocky outcropping near the summit of one of the tallest peaks—Cerro de la Cupula, which has an elevation of 9286 feet above sea level. The observatory's main telescope is housed in a tall cylindrical building with a domed roof. The building is painted a clean white color with sky blue trim and stands out from the muted colors of the forest around it. I wasn't really sure what to expect, but I envisioned the actual observatory being bigger. The building looked more like a water tower or grain silo, only about fifty feet in diameter and maybe four stories tall.

We all parked around the base, and students began to pour out of the bus. Santiago told us to enjoy the view and wander around the outside for a few minutes while he took care of some business. With that he jumped back in his truck and roared down the mountain. The view was fantastic and we could see for miles.

To the east the mountains dropped away steeply, and we could pick out dirt roads that crisscrossed the desert. Highway 3 cut a straight dark line across the valley floor as it made its way to San Felipe. On the distant horizon, the dull blue of the Sea of Cortez was visible as it melted into the lighter blue of the sky. To the west the rocky ridgelines of nearby peaks obscured the panoramic view of the coastal plain, but we could peer down the steep canyons to the hazy foothills below. Haze obscured the western horizon and made it difficult to determine if we were actually seeing the Pacific or just the blue of the sky. The wind whipped over the cold granite, and we had to return to the car to put our fleeces back on.

Soon Santiago returned and gathered the group together. He welcomed us all to the National Observatory and began the tour. He gave a brief history of the observatory and then led us into a small door at the base of the tower. It was dim and musty inside the narrow hallway, and the fake wood veneer on the walls took me back several decades. Santiago led the group to the foot of a spiral staircase and told us to watch our step. We climbed around and around, single file, making our way higher and higher. At the top the staircase opened up to the room that housed the telescope.

The telescope was massive and took up the majority of the room. It was nothing like I imagined it would be. It looked more like a large trash compactor than a telescope. The telescope body was suspended in a heavy framework of blue metal rails and supports, and thick electrical cables trailed below. The actual telescope body was painted a bright yellow and was as wide as it was tall. The telescope used several lenses in conjunction, the largest lens 83 inches in diameter, to enable the viewer to see the actual image. A special computer allowed the astronomers to input the coordinates of the part of space they wished to view. Santiago gave a ten-minute lecture on how the telescope worked and the day-to-day operation of the observatory.

Of course the lecture was in Spanish, so I had to quietly translate for Kat as best I could. It was very interesting and I learned several new things. According to Santiago this observatory is one of the premier places in the world to observe heavenly bodies. He explained that they can observe 98% of the time due to lack of cloud cover. It's rare to have cloud cover overhead because wind flows inward from the two coasts and hits the steep mountains, which creates a constant high pressure system over the mountaintops. This high pressure system prevents any cloud cover from lingering over the ridges. He also told us that the lack of light pollution makes this an ideal spot.

While he admitted that this isn't one of the largest telescopes in the world, it is special because of its versatility. This versatility draws astronomers from around the world to come and use it. He mentioned that the telescope is in use every night and that it is booked solid for years in advance.

The lecture was very educational, and we felt lucky to have stumbled into this extended tour. Once the lecture was over, the students got to have a question and answer period. After the students asked their questions, we made our way outside and walked around the catwalk that went around the top story. It was only a few feet wide with a thin metal railing separating us from the four-story drop-off. It was cool to walk around the outside of the tower and get a 360-degree view.

We all filed back in and headed down the spiral staircase. The tour was now complete. We thanked Santiago again for the tour and his hospitality. Our visit to the National Observatory was fun, informative, and well worth the effort. We got back into truck, and I put it in first gear for our descent down to the valley. We slowly rolled down the steep switchbacks to the main road that went through the park. We drove through the scraggly pines and back toward the park's entrance, where we waved to the ranger on our way out.

We took our time descending the mountain, going slowly and stopping to take several pictures. The haze had finally burned off, and we could see out to the Pacific Ocean now. The temperature rose as we dropped lower and lower, and soon we were back to short sleeves. We rolled down the windows and let the warm breeze circulate through the truck. The trip to Parque National and National Observatory was a great experience, and we left feeling content.

It was around noon when we turned back onto Highway 1, and we were ready for some lunch. We stopped at an open-air roadside restaurant and ordered lunch. Kat tried something new by ordering a fish torta. It turns out this is a type of sandwich made with fry bread. The food was tasty, cheap, and arrived quickly— all good things when you are on the road.

During lunch we found out that despite what the guidebooks said, the people of Baja *do* celebrate Cinco de Mayo. It turns out that it is one of the major holidays that is celebrated during the year. All the kids in school have several days off, and most of the adults don't have to work. The girl behind the counter told us that most people get at least three days off from work and school, so it turns into a six-day weekend. This explained the increase in traffic and people out and about.

In light of this knowledge, we decided to try and find a nice remote place to spend the night away from all the other people who would be out recreating. With this in mind, we pulled out the map and started looking for a good spot. Near the town of San Vicente we found a turn-off that then made its way out to the coast. The area looked like it shouldn't be too crowded, so we decided to head that direction.

We passed through San Vicente and found the turn-off we were looking for. The first ten miles or so were paved, but the road was in pretty bad condition. It had major potholes and was slowly breaking apart. Many of the potholes were filled in with hard packed dirt instead of asphalt. This seemed to be a good short-term solution, and the bumping and jarring was minimal. The pavement ended in a graded dirt road, and we made good time out to the coast.

We passed through the small fishing village of Puerto San Isidro before continuing up the coast. Puerto San Isidro is a small town with a single street and a few houses on either side. The road followed the coastal bluffs, and we passed an occasional cluster of small houses and fish camps. We found a beautiful cove with patches of yellow and orange wildflowers on the bluff above, and it would have made a great camping spot, but alas, there was too much soft beach sand and we decided not to risk it.

We continued along and a few minutes later found a low grassy plain with a nice beach below. It was still early afternoon and we weren't sure if it was time to camp yet, but we definitely needed to spend some time on the beach. We walked down to the beach and plopped ourselves in the sand, smelling the salt and feeling the cool onshore breeze.

There were some nice sets of waves rolling in, so we ran back to the truck and pulled off the kayak. Changing into our swimsuits, we gathered the paddles and seats and got ready to play around in the water. We knew that we would soon be back to the more populated northern areas of Baja and this might be our last time to play in the surf.

Paddling out, I screamed like a little girl as the first wave sloshed over the bow and hit me full in the chest. Gasping for air, I pretended that I liked the cold water and gritted my teeth. The cold water wasn't nearly as bad after getting eaten by a wave or two, and soon I didn't even notice it. The kayak was still pulling the same old tricks of turning sideways and digging in the nose, and I ended up swimming after the kayak most of the time. Kat and I took turns with the kayak for an hour or two till the waves started diminishing, and then we washed ashore, tired and wet. We lay in the wet sand, watching waves roll in for a while, before getting ready to leave.

Back at the truck I filled the sun shower again, knowing that I would be feeling sticky by the time we reached camp. We found a nice spot to camp a few miles up the road. It was about halfway down the bluff on a nice level spot overlooking a rock outcropping that stuck out into the sea. The road leading down to camp was kind of rough, but I gave it my tried and true method of lots of gas and bounced on through without any problem. I was a teensy bit worried about getting back up the hill in the morning, but I figured I would worry about it then.

The campsite was far enough below the main road to give us some privacy, and we had the place to ourselves. The surf crashed below us, and there was a small trail that led down to some tide pools. We found a nice level spot for the truck and lay the sun shower out to heat up.

Not wanting to set up camp quite yet, we shirked our responsibilities and wandered down the trail to explore the tide pools. The tide pools were full of hermit crabs, sea anemones, and starfish, but the tide was coming in and we soon had to retreat or be swept off the rocks.

We walked back up the trail and started to unload the truck and set up camp. The solar shower was warm enough now, so we took quick showers and started looking through our food Tupperware for dinner. Our food supply was pretty slim since this would be our last dinner in Baja. Kat rummaged around and pulled out some dented cup-o-noodles, saltines, and a dehydrated backpacking food packet — a dinner fit for a king.

We slurped our noodles, sat looking out at the water, and watched the sun sink below the waves. It was a beautiful sunset, like so many others we had experienced during our travels in Baja. It was sad to think that by the time the sun set again tomorrow we would be back across the border.

One thing that made it easier for us to accept that the trip was coming to an end was that we felt like we had already left the "real" Baja behind. The vast expanses of cactus filled desert and the white sand beaches with warm clear water were hundreds of miles south. The hot, dry, scrubby Baja that stole our hearts had transformed into a temperate, green, and populated place.

The allure of the unknown that had drawn us to Baja had been replaced with the satisfaction of discovery, and it was now time to go home. Fifteen days on the road can make even the hardiest of adventurers look forward to a hot shower and a soft bed.

Day 16

When the soft pitter-patter of raindrops falling awakened me in the predawn hours, I did what most experienced campers would do: I rolled over and hoped the rain would stop soon and that we wouldn't get too wet. A few hours later Kat woke me up with a nudge as the sun rose, and we watched our last Baja sunrise still snuggled deep in our damp sleeping bags. We laughed that our only rain during the trip had been on the last day—figures.

The rain clouds had dissipated, and only large cotton candy puffs of clouds remained. It looked like it would be a nice day, and the sun was already drying out our sleeping bags. After breakfast I was just sitting around thinking about getting ready for the day when I noticed several dolphins swimming about twenty yards off shore. We pulled out the binoculars and watched them leap and dive for several minutes until they disappeared for good. It was a good omen on our last day in Baja.

Packing up the truck one final time, we tried to get an early start on the day. As we put the last of the items away, I started to remember that I might have a tough time getting back up to the road. There was a particularly steep spot with deep ruts that I was a little concerned about.

I had Kat get out and try to direct my wheel placement so I didn't get stuck. That worked out fine, but once I got moving I was nervous about losing my momentum and nearly ran Kat over as she was trying to cross back to the passenger side. She jumped out of the way to avoid getting run over, but a few choice words were exchanged when she opened the door and climbed back inside. Nobody likes to get run over.

The coastal road continued northward and eventually looped back to the highway, but it was marked as unimproved dirt on the map, and we didn't feel like taking a chance on its condition this late in the game. We had done really well on the trip and didn't want to spoil it on the last day by getting stuck. So we turned back the way we had come and backtracked out to the highway.

Our next destination was Punta Banda. This was about forty miles up the coast near Ensenada. We had visited Punta Banda on our first trip to Baja several years ago and were familiar with the area. Punta Banda is the peninsula that forms the lower part of Bahía Todos Santos and is a popular tourist destination.

Out on the tip of the peninsula is an attraction called the Buffadora. It is a blowhole where the ocean swell is forced up through a natural cavity in the rock. With a great rushing sound, the hole emits a fountain of water thirty feet high into the air. This natural wonder has been thoroughly commercialized and turned into a huge tourist attraction. Even though we knew it might be crowded due to the holiday, we decided to risk it and visit anyway.

It took us an hour or so to reach the Buffadora's parking area. We were quickly accosted by a parking attendant/hustler and directed into a parking lot. These guys stand in the middle of the roadway and act official, directing traffic this way and that. At first it seems like they are just being helpful, until you realize that they are steering people away from the cheaper public parking area to their particular parking lot.

They are very adamant in their signaling of traffic, and I am sure many tourists don't even realize that they have a choice to park somewhere else. I remembered this parking trick from the time before, but the attendant was so loud and pushy that I figured it was easier to pay the few dollars than to try to fight it.

To reach the Buffadora you have to walk down a narrow lane with shops of all types on either side. We were some of the first tourists to arrive, and the street was mostly empty. The vendors were sleepily pulling up the roll-up doors and placing their wares out on display. A few of them gave a halfhearted attempt to lure us into their shops, but it was still too early — even for them. We stopped to buy ten pesos worth of churros and munched on them contentedly as we walked toward the Buffadora. You just can't beat fried dough rolled in sugar and cinnamon for breakfast.

The Buffadora was great. There was hardly anyone around, and with each surge of the ocean a huge plume of water rocketed up into the sky with a loud whoosh. We snapped pictures of each of us getting covered in the salty mist. The sun had burned through the early morning cloud cover by now, and we sat on a bench and admired the view of the coastline. It was a good idea to get there early, because soon crowds of people started arriving. Sensing that it was only going to get more crowded as the day went on, we decided to leave.

Most of the shops were now open, and the vendors were much more awake and ready to try to separate us from our money. There was a huge variety of touristy items being sold: T-shirts, jewelry, carvings of stone and wood, traditional Mexican clothing, stained glass, leather goods, and all manner of other small trinkets. Prices were now quoted in dollars, and several merchants looked at me funny when I bargained using pesos.

It was nearly impossible to make the quarter mile back to the car without being sucked into at least a few shops, but I managed to hold strong and not purchase anything . . . almost. Actually, I did manage to make it all the way past the rows of shops, but then near the parking lot I found myself drawn into a small fireworks place. I had told the boys in my Scout troop back home that I would try to bring them back some fireworks. One hundred pesos poorer, I emerged from the shop with a big bag of fireworks in my hand. Kat just shook her head and made a disparaging comment about giving twelve-year-old boys firecrackers. I don't know what she's talking about — twelve-year-old boys love fireworks.

Grumbling, I paid the parking guy his three dollars and we turned back onto the highway. Just before we reached Highway 1 again, we saw a small stand advertising ice cold coconuts. I asked Kat if she had ever had one and when she shook her head no, I braked hard and swerved over to the side of the road.

Back when I was in Costa Rica I used to drink these all the time, and they were great. We called these unripe coconuts "pépas," and they could be bought from street vendors all over the place. I was excited for Kat to try her first pépa. I got out of the truck and made my way over to the stand. I was greeted by a young kid of only ten or eleven, and he asked in broken English what I wanted to buy. I replied in Spanish, asking how much for a coconut, and was given the inflated tourist price. I laughed and countered with about half the asking price in pesos. He looked unsure and then with a shrug put out his hand for the money. Money in hand he turned, reached into an ancient refrigerator, and pulled out two unripe green coconuts.

Pulling out a machete from under the table, he deftly held the coconut in his left hand and with several quick strokes shaved off most of the top. Now that most of the husk was gone, he took the tip of the machete and bored a small hole in the top.

Sticking a bendy straw in the hole, he handed the coconut over and quickly repeated the process with the second one. I walked back to the truck proudly displaying the coconuts in either hand. Kat was a little unsure of whether or not she wanted to suck the water out of an unripe coconut, but after one sip she was sold. The juice is almost clear and has a mild sweet flavor. I have been told that the juice is packed with vitamins and is very healthy.

We turned back onto the highway, sipping our coconuts and feeling good about our morning activities. We soon reached the junction of Highway 1 and entered the sprawl of Ensenada. It was congested on the highway, and being surrounded by so many unpredictable drivers made me nervous.

It was always a surprise to see what the driver next to you was going to do. Another factor that kept us on our toes was the lack of lane markings and road signs. Suddenly I found myself being passed on the right-hand side by a semi truck that decided the shoulder would work just fine as a passing lane. Before I could react, about ten other cars figured that they would follow the semi's lead, and now the two-lane road simply converted to a three-lane road with a passing lane on the right-hand side.

At one intersection a car in the left-hand turn lane got tired of waiting and decided to pull back into traffic and continue going straight. This would have been okay, if I hadn't been barreling along at 50 mph when he darted into my lane from a complete stop. It was amazing that I managed to brake hard enough to avoid running the car over. Even more amazing to me was the fact that we were so close that I could see that the other driver hadn't even looked in his mirror to see if there was traffic coming before pulling into my lane.

These conditions made for some stressful driving and took all of our concentration just to avoid being hit. I tried to watch cars to our left and Kat to our right. As we entered the more urban areas, we started having to deal with more streetlights and four-way stops.

As I previously mentioned, four-way stops are disastrous. The fact that some drivers stopped, others slowed, and some ignored the stop sign entirely made for some close calls. We were both pretty well frazzled by the time we reached downtown Ensenada, and we couldn't wait to get through the city—away from all the crazy drivers. A quiet desperation came over us as we knew that it was only a matter of time before someone hit us. The sooner we got out, the better our chances of escaping unharmed.

The streets were packed, and we moved slowly across town. The streets were mostly four-lane boulevards with a four-way stop at every block. By now I had determined that the best defense was a strong offense. I started to drive a bit more aggressively — cutting people off, not waiting my turn, and ignoring all the traffic laws known to man. This driving style was much more appropriate for the conditions, and I think the other drivers around me respected me for it. Even still it took complete concentration and a good wingman, or in this case a good wing woman, to avoid being hit.

While sitting at a red light, we licked our dry lips and wanly smiled at each other, savoring the moment. We had driven for thousands of miles all over Baja without an accident, and now with only a hundred miles left, we were scared. The light changed and we cautiously pulled out into the intersection. We almost made it across the intersection when a bus came whipping out around us, inches from clipping our front corner, accelerated, and promptly ran into the stopped car in front of us. The bus didn't even hit the brakes. The unsuspecting car's whole back section was crushed.

Horns blared and we sat frozen, unable to comprehend what had just happened. Stunned, we watched the driver of the car get out, shake his head sadly, and nonchalantly start to talk with the bus driver who was surveying the damage to his front bumper. That was much too close for comfort. It is safe to say that we were both totally freaked out now, and our desire to be out of Ensenada jumped to a whole new level. We pulled around the accident and did everything humanly possible to flee the city as quickly as possible.

Back on the open road north of Ensenada, we let out a huge sigh of relief and vowed to never drive through Ensenada again. We passed the turnoff for Highway 3 that we had taken to San Felipe, now completing the loop that we had started more than two weeks ago.

Earlier that morning we decided that instead of dealing with the crowds and crossing at Tijuana, we would take Highway 3 north and cross the border in Tecate. The other factor that influenced our decision to cross at Tecate was that we had never traveled the northern stretch of Highway 3 and wanted to see what it had to offer.

We soon reached the turnoff and exited Highway 1 for the last time. The drive on Highway 3 took us through rolling hills and over several mountain passes. Large vineyards with their endless rows of grapes filled the valleys, and every so often there was a sign with an arrow pointing down a dirt road, advertising wine tasting. As we made our way northward, the hills flattened and the vineyards were replaced by large fields of grain and pastures filled with cows. The wind was cool and a few raindrops splattered on the hood of the truck as we drove along.

It was now midafternoon, and we were ready for some lunch. We pulled out the trusty guidebooks and looked for a good restaurant. Tecate was only a few miles away now, and we wanted to eat as soon a possible. Counting our remaining pesos, we determined that we could splurge a little and eat somewhere nice. The plan was to try to spend all of our remaining pesos before crossing back into the United States.

We selected a place called The Mission, and after making a wrong turn or two finally found it. This was by far the fanciest restaurant we had been to, and we were woefully underdressed. Not minding a bit, we went inside and had lunch. The food and service were great, and it was fun to be in such a nice restaurant after fifteen days of camping. I'm sure we got a few strange looks, but we didn't care. We ended up spending almost all of our pesos, and we were now ready to brave the border crossing.

We were a little nervous about crossing the border and weren't sure what to expect. Our truck was packed with stuff, and I wasn't sure if they were going to ask a lot of questions or want to unload things to look for contraband.

First off, we had to find the border crossing, which proved to be more of a challenge than I thought it would be. Apparently there was some serious road construction being done to the road leading to the crossing. There were signs along the way indicating that we would have to follow a detour to reach the border crossing.

In classic Baja style, the detour signs didn't actually lead us to the border crossing. Instead, we soon found ourselves driving around in a dead-end neighborhood near the border. We could see the border only a few hundred feet away but couldn't manage to find a way to get there. I guess it was fitting that we got lost getting into the country and then lost again trying to leave.

We finally had a lucky break and turned down an unmarked street that led us to the crossing station. We waited in line for about five minutes and pulled up to the window. Crossing the border was a snap, and all our worries were unfounded. All we had to do was flash our driver's licenses, answer a question or two, and off we went. Before we knew it we were back in the United States of America. Wow, we had done it—driven the whole length of the Baja Peninsula and made it back in one piece to tell about it.

Reflection

Our Baja road trip was an epic journey and quite the adventure in more ways than one. Quite simply, Baja exceeded all of our hopes and expectations. Looking back at the trip, the few magical weeks we spent traveling in Baja have created memories that will last a lifetime. It was a great adventure for us, and we hope it won't be our last.

During our travels across Baja, we were granted the chance to discover new and beautiful places that we wouldn't have ever known existed otherwise. Baja is contagious, and it only took a little bit for me to get hooked. Its rugged landscape and beautiful coastline were a wonderful change from the long cold winter. Baja's empty beaches and solitude helped us to relax and made it possible to settle into a more natural pace of life. This sixteen-day trip was the ultimate escape from the material aspects of our life — all we needed to survive and thrive fit into our truck. As our lives were simplified, it became easier to concentrate on what was really important.

The whole process of being inspired with an idea, planning it out, and *actually* doing it has made it clear in my mind that even after starting a career and settling down into "real life," adventures are still possible. This realization has made the return to real life much more tolerable, because I know that there will always be something to look forward to — it's just a matter of dreaming it up.

Adventures and dreams come in all shapes and sizes, but this experience taught me that they need to be nourished or they will fade away. By seizing this opportunity, it has ensured that in the years to come we will continue to dream, plan, and actually do the things that we daydream about.

One of the best parts of this trip for me was the quality time that Kat and I got to spend together. It reminded me of the old days when we used to run the river. We had such a good time spending our first few summers together, living and guiding on the Colorado River. These summers gave us a lot of time to get to know each other and learn to work as a team and formed the foundation of our relationship.

This trip was the most time we had spent together, one on one, since our summer in Alaska. It was fun to be able hang out together full time and share in the Baja experience. It had been too long since we had had a good adventure with just the two of us, and it was nice to re-cement our bonds after taking some time off to do school and real jobs.

While driving through San Diego on our way home, we already found ourselves talking about our next Baja trip. In the few weeks that we spent down there, we saw only a fraction of the peninsula and it left us wanting more. One could spend months traveling and exploring and not see it all. We talked of certain friends and family who would love such a trip, and we got excited about the prospect of bringing them with us next time. Will it happen? Yes, I'd like to think so. Baja gets in your blood, and it is only a matter of time before you find yourself longing to return. I am already feeling the pull of the open road, and we hope to go back soon.

The adjustment back into real life after returning from Baja was surprisingly smooth. Shortly after returning home, we packed our bags and left for a river trip in eastern Utah. It was go, go, go, all summer, and our busy schedules never left us any time to catch our breath. Somehow I managed to sandwich enough days of work between vacations to keep my job, and before we knew it the summer was over.

As the fall leaves began to turn, I found myself settling back into the comfortable yet vaguely unsatisfying routine of real life—back to work and responsibilities. The memories of Baja seemed far away and were starting to get fuzzy until one day I pulled out the journal and started to read. I found myself longing to return and just sit on the beach and soak up the sun. Before long I found myself sitting in front of the computer, plunking out the story of our Baja adventure.

It's winter again and I find myself getting antsy. What is it about wintertime anyway? I'm not sure if it's a blessing or a curse, but winter always makes me a little bit crazy. Reliving the Baja experience by writing this book has helped calm my inner unrest, but I still find myself daydreaming of faraway places and adventures just waiting to happen.

Priorities change, as I am finding out with the birth of our first son, Carson, but my desire to see the world firsthand hasn't diminished any. If anything, I am excited to inspire him to have as many wonderful experiences and adventures as possible. A young baby may slow us down this spring, but there is always next year. Ahhh yes . . . next year.